THE SCIENCE OF
HABITS

WHY WE DO WHAT WE DO AND HOW TO CHANGE IT?

Three-Step Process to Analyze Your Habits and Change Them.

ADARSH GUPTA, DO

Contents

Disclaimer

The information provided in this book, "The Science of Habits: Why We Do What We Do and How to Change It," is intended for informational purposes only. It is not intended to be a substitute for professional medical advice, diagnosis, or treatment. Always seek the advice of your physician or other qualified health provider with any questions you may have regarding a medical condition.

The author and publisher of this book have made every effort to ensure that the information presented is accurate and up to date. However, they make no representations or warranties of any kind, express or implied, about the completeness, accuracy, reliability, suitability, or availability of the information contained in this book. Any reliance you place on such information is strictly at your own risk.

The book may discuss general principles and strategies for habits and behavior change, but individual circumstances may vary. Therefore, it is important to consult with a qualified healthcare professional or specialist before making any significant changes to your habits or behavior.

The author and publisher are not responsible for any loss, injury, or damage incurred as a result of the information provided in this book. This includes but is not limited to direct, indirect, consequential, or incidental damages arising out of the use or misuse of the information presented.

Remember, the content in this book should not be considered a substitute for professional medical advice, diagnosis, or treatment. Always seek the guidance of a qualified healthcare professional with any questions or concerns you may have regarding your health or specific medical condition.

By reading this book, you acknowledge and agree to the terms and conditions of this medical disclaimer.

Mention of specific brand-name products, mobile apps, companies, organizations, or authorities in this book does not imply endorsement by the author, nor does mention of specific brand-name products, medical apps, companies, organizations, or authorities imply that they endorse this book, its author, or the publisher. The brand-name products mentioned in this book are trademarks or registered trademarks of their respective companies.

Internet addresses given in this book were accurate at the time it went to press.

Although the author and publisher have made every effort to ensure that the information in this book was correct at press time, the author and publisher do not assume and hereby disclaim any liability to any party for any loss, damage, or disruption caused by errors or omissions, whether such errors or omissions result from negligence, accident, or any other cause.

Adherence to all applicable laws and regulations, including international, federal, state, and local governing professional licensing, business practices, advertising, and all other aspects of doing business in the US, Canada, or any other jurisdiction, is the sole responsibility of the reader and consumer.

Neither the author nor the publisher assumes any responsibility or liability whatsoever on behalf of the consumer or reader of this material. Any perceived slight of any individual or organization is purely unintentional.

The resources in this book are provided for informational purposes only. They should not be used to replace the specialized training and professional judgment of a health care or mental health care professional.

For more information, email contact@adarshgupta.com.

Introduction

"Your habits will determine your future. Make them count."

A habit is a behavior that is automatic, repetitive, and learned through experience, and it is a fundamental part of human behavior[1]. These behaviors are typically executed without much conscious thought, allowing individuals to conserve mental energy and reduce cognitive load. Habits can be both positive and negative and can significantly impact an individual's overall health and well-being[2].

The concept of habits has been studied extensively by researchers across various disciplines, including psychology, neuroscience, and sociology.

Habits are formed through a process known as *neuroplasticity*, which involves the strengthening of neural connections in the brain through repeated behavior. When a behavior is repeated, the neural pathways associated with that behavior become stronger, making it easier for the behavior to be repeated in the future. This process is reinforced by the release of dopamine, a neurotransmitter that plays a key role in motivation and reward. The release of dopamine in response to a behavior reinforces the behavior and makes it more likely to be repeated in the future.

In addition to neuroplasticity and dopamine, conditioning contributes to habit formation. *Conditioning* involves associating behavior with a particular environmental stimulus or context. For example, if an individual habitually eats a snack while watching TV, the act of watching TV becomes a cue for the behavior of eating a snack. This type of conditioning can be particularly powerful in shaping habitual behavior, as the environmental cues become integrated with the behavior itself, making it difficult to break the habit.

Habits can become so deeply ingrained that they are almost second nature, requiring little conscious effort or attention to perform, such as brushing your teeth before bed. This habit is deeply ingrained because it has been repeated consistently over a long period, often since childhood. The trigger of completing the evening routine becomes associated with the craving for cleanliness and oral hygiene, leading to the action of brushing teeth and the subsequent reward.

Positive habits, such as regular exercise, healthy eating, and good sleep hygiene, can have a profound impact on our physical and mental health. They can improve our mood, increase energy levels, reduce stress and anxiety, and prevent chronic diseases such as obesity, diabetes, and cardiovascular disease. In contrast, negative habits such as smoking, excessive alcohol consumption, and procrastination can have detrimental effects on our health, relationships, and work performance.

Habits can also be influenced by a range of internal and external factors. Childhood experiences, social norms, cultural expectations, and peer pressure can all play a role in shaping our habits. Genetic factors may also contribute to the development of habits, with research indicating that some individuals may be more predisposed to developing addictive behaviors than others.

Changing habits can be challenging, as they are deeply ingrained and often automatic. However, with practice and persistence, it is possible to modify existing habits and develop new ones. This process often involves identifying the cue, routine, and reward associated with the habit and making targeted changes to one or more of these elements. It can also involve practicing mindful awareness, setting achievable goals, and rewarding oneself for positive behaviors.

In summary, habit is a behavior that is automatic, repetitive, and learned through experience, and it is a fundamental part of human behavior. Habits are integral to our daily lives, influencing our thoughts, feelings, and behaviors. They can be either positive or negative, depending on their impact on our health and well-being. Understanding the science of habit formation and change can help individuals develop healthy habits and overcome negative ones. With practice and persistence, it is possible to make lasting changes that promote a happier, healthier, and more fulfilling life.

Importance of habits

Habits are important because they play a significant role in shaping our daily lives and routines. They play a crucial role in everyday life, as they can help individuals conserve energy and reduce cognitive load by automating routine behaviors. For example, brushing our teeth or putting on a seatbelt become automatic behaviors that we don't have to think about consciously.

In addition to simplifying our daily routines, habits are also important in shaping health-related behaviors. For example, individuals who develop regular exercise habits are more likely to maintain an active lifestyle, reducing their risk of chronic diseases such as obesity, diabetes, and cardiovascular disease. Similarly, individuals who develop healthy eating habits are more likely to maintain a balanced and nutritious diet, improving their overall health and well-being[2].

Habits can also significantly impact our mental health, with research indicating that individuals who develop positive habits such as meditation or gratitude journaling can experience reduced stress and improved mood. Conversely, negative habits such as excessive alcohol consumption or procrastination can have detrimental effects on our mental health, contributing to anxiety and depression.

Furthermore, habits can be valuable targets for behavior change interventions. Research has shown that habitual behaviors are more likely to be maintained over time, making them a valuable target for behavior change interventions[1].

Individuals can significantly improve their physical and mental health, relationships, work performance, and overall quality of life by developing positive habits and breaking negative ones.

Overview of the book

This book will explore the science of habits, including how habits form, why we do what we do, and how to change habits. The book will draw on evidence-based research from psychology, neuroscience, and other fields to provide practical strategies for individuals who wish to develop healthier habits.

CHAPTER SUMMARY

Habits are important because they simplify our daily routines, shape health-related behaviors, and significantly impact our physical and mental health. Developing positive habits and breaking negative ones can be valuable tools for promoting lasting behavior change and improving overall well-being.

Chapter 1: The Science of Habit Formation

"We are what we repeatedly do. Excellence, then, is not an act but a habit." - Aristotle.

Habit formation is a complex process involving various psychological and neural mechanisms. Research in the habit formation field has identified several key factors that influence how habits are formed and maintained.

One of the most important factors in habit formation is *repetition*. Studies have shown that repeated behavior is more likely to become automatic and habitual over time. This is because repetition strengthens the connections between neural pathways, making it easier for the brain to execute the behavior without conscious effort[3].

Another critical factor in habit formation is the role of *rewards*. The brain is wired to seek out rewards and positive outcomes, and behaviors that are associated with positive outcomes are more likely to become habitual. For example, a person who enjoys the rush of endorphins from running may be more likely to develop a habit of running regularly[4].

However, not all rewards are equal in their ability to promote habit formation. Research has shown that immediate rewards are more effective than delayed rewards in promoting habit formation. This is because the brain is wired to prioritize immediate rewards over delayed ones, and behaviors that are associated with immediate rewards are more likely to become habitual[5].

Immediate rewards are more effective than delayed rewards in promoting habit formation.

The timing and consistency of rewards are also important factors in habit formation. Studies have shown that consistently rewarded behaviors are more likely to become habits than inconsistently rewarded[6]. Additionally, research has demonstrated that intermittent reinforcement, in which rewards are given unpredictably, can be particularly effective in promoting habit formation[7].

Consistently rewarded behaviors are more likely to become habits than inconsistently rewarded.

Another important factor in habit formation is the context in which the behavior occurs. *Contextual cues*, such as the time of day, location, or social setting, can trigger habitual behaviors. For example, a person may habitually reach for a cigarette when they are in a particular social setting, such as a bar or party. These contextual cues can be particularly powerful in triggering automatic behaviors[8].

Contextual cues can trigger habitual behaviors.

Finally, the process of habit formation is influenced by a range of individual differences, including genetic factors, personality traits, and cognitive styles. For example, research has shown that individuals with a strong "behavioral activation" personality trait, characterized by high levels of energy and enthusiasm, are more likely to develop positive habits such as exercise[9]. Additionally, studies have suggested that genetic factors may play a role in developing habits, with specific genes being associated with addictive behaviors[10].

In summary, habit formation is a complex process influenced by various psychological and neural mechanisms. The key factors in habit formation include repetition, rewards, context, and individual differences. Understanding these factors can be valuable in promoting positive habit formation and breaking negative ones.

The Habit Cycle

Charles Duhigg described the habit loop as a three-step process that governs the formation and maintenance of habits. The loop begins with a cue or trigger, which signals the brain to initiate a particular behavior. The behavior is then followed by a reward, reinforcing it and making it more likely to be repeated in the future. Over time, the habit becomes automatic and can be triggered by the cue without conscious thought or effort. This process is supported by research on habit formation, which has shown that habits are stored in a different part of the brain than deliberate, goal-directed actions[3].

However, there is one more step that is crucial in this three-step process, and that is *craving*. So, in fact, the habit loop is a four-step process. We will call it *"The Habit Cycle"*(Figure 1). Let's learn each step in a little more detail.

Step 1. Trigger

The first step is the trigger, which is the *cue or signal that prompts the habit*. Triggers are the first step in the habit cycle and can take many forms. They are the cue or signal that initiates the habit cycle and can be internal or external. Identifying triggers is essential for changing habits because it allows individuals to recognize the cues that prompt the unwanted behavior and develop strategies to avoid or cope with them. An external trigger could be a particular location, such as a coffee shop or a bar, that prompts the habit of drinking coffee or alcohol. A time of day can also be an external trigger, such as the morning coffee or the evening TV habit. Internal triggers can be emotions, such as anxiety or boredom, that lead to the habit of snacking or smoking. For example, someone who habitually snacks when they feel anxious might feel a sudden urge to eat when they experience an anxiety-provoking event.

Step 2. Craving

The second step is the craving, which is the *psychological response to the trigger*. Cravings create a sense of anticipation and desire for the habit to be enacted. Cravings can take many forms and can be both physical and psychological. For example, someone who habitually drinks coffee might experience a physical craving in the form of a headache if they skip their morning cup. They might also experience a psychological craving, such as a feeling of comfort or energy that they associate with the ritual of drinking coffee. Similarly, someone who habitually smokes might experience physical cravings in the form of nicotine withdrawal symptoms and psychological cravings, such as a feeling of relaxation or stress relief that they associate with smoking. Understanding the nature of cravings is crucial for changing unwanted habits because it allows individuals to identify the internal mechanisms that drive the habit and develop strategies to manage or redirect the craving.

Step 3. Action

The third step is the action, which is the behavior itself that is triggered by the craving. *Actions are the observable manifestation of the habit.* For example, someone who habitually bites their nails might begin the action of nail-biting when they feel a sudden urge to do so. Similarly, someone who habitually checks their phone might begin the action of scrolling through social media when they feel a moment of boredom. Actions can also be more complex, such as the habit of procrastination, which might involve a series of mental and physical actions, such as avoiding tasks, engaging in distracting activities, and postponing deadlines. Understanding the nature of actions is critical for changing unwanted habits because it allows individuals to identify the specific behaviors that need to be modified or replaced to break the habit cycle.

Step 4. Reward

Finally, the *reward is the positive outcome that reinforces the habit cycle and makes it more likely to occur again in the future*. Rewards can be tangible, such as the pleasure of eating a favorite food or the feeling of relaxation that comes with smoking a cigarette. They can also be intangible, such as the sense of accomplishment that comes with completing a task or the feeling of connection that comes with checking social media. *Rewards are critical for forming and maintaining habits because they create a sense of pleasure or satisfaction that reinforces the habit cycle.* For example, someone who habitually eats junk food might experience the reward of a pleasurable taste sensation or a temporary feeling of fullness. Similarly, someone who habitually procrastinates might experience the reward of a temporary feeling of relief or a sense of avoidance of a difficult task. Understanding the nature of rewards is essential for changing unwanted habits because it allows individuals to identify the underlying motivations that reinforce the habit and develop strategies to replace the reward with a more positive and sustainable alternative.

Understanding the habit cycle and the role of each step in forming habits is essential for changing unwanted habits and developing new, healthier ones.

One key aspect of the habit cycle is the role of rewards in shaping behavior. Rewards can be positive, such as the pleasure derived from eating a tasty snack, or negative, such as the relief from pain or discomfort that comes from taking a painkiller. In either case, the reward reinforces the behavior that preceded it and strengthens the habit. However, the timing of the reward is also crucial, as research has shown that *immediate rewards are more effective at promoting habit formation than delayed rewards*[5].

Immediate rewards are more effective at promoting habit than delayed rewards.

The Science of Habits

Figure 1. The Habit Cycle.

Another important factor in the habit loop is the concept of future self-continuity or the degree to which an individual sees their future self as connected to their present self. Research has shown that individuals who have a stronger sense of future self-continuity are more likely to engage in behaviors that benefit their future selves, such as saving money or exercising regularly[6].

Understanding the habit cycle can be helpful for individuals who want to change their habits, as it provides a framework for identifying and modifying the triggers, cravings, actions, and rewards that contribute to the habit. For example, individuals can try replacing an unhealthy behavior, such as snacking on junk food when bored, with a healthier alternative, such as taking a walk or doing a crossword puzzle, that provides a similar reward[7]. Additionally, making minor changes to the cues that trigger the craving, such as avoiding certain locations or activities that prompt the craving, can also be effective[8].

In summary, the habit cycle is a four-step process that governs the formation and maintenance of habits. The cycle involves a trigger, a craving, an action, and a reward and is supported by research on habit formation and behavior change. Understanding the habit cycle can be helpful for individuals who want to change their habits and develop healthier, more productive behaviors.

How are Habits Formed?

Habits are formed through a process of reinforcement learning in the brain that involves the formation of neural pathways that connect cues, cravings, actions, and rewards. The basal ganglia, a region of the brain associated with motor control and habit formation, plays a crucial role in this process. When a person is exposed to a particular cue, such as the smell of coffee, it triggers a craving in the basal ganglia, which initiates a sequence of behavior (action) that leads to the reward, such as the pleasurable taste of the coffee. Over time, the repeated activation of this cue-craving-action-reward sequence strengthens the neural pathways associated with the habit, making it more automatic and less subject to conscious control.

Studies have shown that the timing and consistency of the rewards are critical factors in forming habits. In one study, rats were trained to press a lever to receive a food reward. When the reward was delivered immediately after the lever was pressed, the rats quickly learned the behavior and formed a habit. However, when the reward was delayed, the rats were less likely to form a habit and showed more variability in their behavior. Similarly, human studies have shown that consistent rewards form stronger habits than intermittent rewards.

Understanding how habits are formed is essential for changing unwanted habits because it allows individuals to identify the specific cues, cravings, actions, and rewards that contribute to the habit loop and develop strategies to modify or replace them. By altering the cue or changing the reward, individuals can weaken the neural pathways associated with the habit and create new pathways that reinforce more positive behaviors.

Neuroplasticity and Habit Formation

Neuroplasticity refers to the brain's ability to change and adapt in response to experiences and environmental factors. It is a crucial process involved in habit formation because it allows the brain to modify its neural pathways in response to repeated behavior patterns. Research has shown that habitual behavior leads to changes in the brain's structure and function, strengthening neural connections associated with the habit and weakening connections associated with alternative behaviors.

One study by Graybiel et al. (2000)[11] demonstrated the role of neuroplasticity in habit formation by examining the neural activity of rats trained to perform a lever-pressing task for a reward. The researchers found that after repeated training, the rats exhibited a shift in neural activity from the striatum, a region of the brain associated with goal-directed behavior, to the dorsolateral striatum, an area associated with habitual behavior.

Furthermore, studies have shown that neuroplasticity is a two-way process, and the brain can undergo both positive and negative changes in response to experiences. For example, research by Hölzel et al. (2012)[12] found that practicing mindfulness meditation can lead to increases in gray matter density in the prefrontal cortex, a region of the brain associated with self-regulation and emotional control. In contrast, excessive alcohol consumption has been shown to shrink gray matter in the prefrontal cortex, contributing to impaired decision-making and self-control[13].

Understanding the role of neuroplasticity in habit formation is essential for changing unwanted habits because it highlights the potential for the brain to adapt and change in response to new experiences and behaviors. Individuals can create new neural pathways that reinforce positive habits and weaken the neural pathways associated with unwanted habits by promoting neuroplasticity, such as learning new skills or practicing mindfulness.

In conclusion, neuroplasticity plays a critical role in habit formation, with repeated patterns of behavior leading to changes in the brain's structure and function. Understanding the mechanisms of neuroplasticity provides insights into the potential for positive change and underscores the importance of sustained effort and repetition in habit formation. By promoting neuroplasticity through positive experiences and behaviors, individuals can modify their neural pathways and reinforce more positive habits.

Dopamine and Habit Formation

Dopamine is a neurotransmitter that plays a critical role in reward processing and reinforcement learning, including the formation of habits. Research has shown that dopamine release in response to rewarding stimuli, such as food or drugs, reinforces the behavior that led to the reward and strengthens the neural pathways associated with that behavior.

One study by Yin et al. (2006)[14] demonstrated the role of dopamine in habit formation by examining the neural activity of rats trained to run through a maze to obtain a reward. The researchers found that after repeated training, the rats exhibited a shift in neural activity from the dorsomedial striatum, a region of the brain associated with goal-directed behavior, to the dorsolateral striatum, an area associated with habitual behavior. Furthermore, the researchers found that dopamine signaling in the dorsolateral striatum was critical for forming habitual behavior.

Other studies have shown that dopamine release is essential for forming habits related to drug addiction. For example, research by Volkow and colleagues (2006)[15] found that repeated cocaine use led to increased dopamine release in the dorsolateral striatum, contributing to the development of habitual drug-seeking behavior. Furthermore, the researchers found that reducing dopamine signaling in the dorsolateral striatum decreased the rats' drug-seeking behavior, highlighting the importance of dopamine signaling in habit formation related to drug addiction.

Understanding the role of dopamine in habit formation is essential for changing unwanted habits because it highlights the potential for reinforcement and reward-based learning to shape behavior. Individuals can modify their neural pathways and reinforce positive habits by reducing exposure to rewarding stimuli and engaging in activities promoting dopamine release.

In conclusion, dopamine plays a critical role in habit formation, with reinforcement and reward-based learning shaping behavior through strengthening neural pathways associated with habitual behavior. By promoting dopamine release through positive experiences and behaviors, individuals can modify their neural pathways and reinforce more positive habits. Understanding the mechanisms of dopamine signaling provides insights into the potential for positive change and underscores the importance of sustained effort and repetition in habit formation.

Conditioning and Habit Formation

Conditioning refers to the process by which behavior is learned through repeated associations with a particular stimulus or context. Research has shown that conditioning plays a critical role in forming habits, with repeated exposure to a specific trigger leading to automatic and unconscious responses.

One study by Lally and colleagues (2010)[1] investigated the formation of habits through a 12-week study of health behaviors in which participants reported their behavior and the associated context for each behavior. The researchers found that participants' initial intention to perform a behavior was a strong predictor of behavior during the first weeks of the study. However, after an average of 66 days, participants reported that the behavior became automatic and required less cognitive effort, suggesting the formation of a habit.

Classical conditioning is a process by which we learn to associate a neutral stimulus with a response that is naturally triggered by another stimulus. This type of learning can contribute to habit formation by creating a powerful association between a cue and behavior. For example, if someone consistently eats a sweet treat while watching TV, they may start to associate the sight of the TV with the pleasure of eating the treat. Over time, this association can become so strong that the person automatically reaches for the treat whenever they sit down to watch TV, even if they are not hungry or do not consciously intend to eat the treat. In this way, classical conditioning can help to establish the cues and triggers that drive habits. Similarly, research (Hyman 2001)[16] has shown that individuals with drug addiction may develop conditioned responses to drug-related stimuli, contributing to the formation of habitual drug-seeking behavior.

Understanding the role of conditioning in habit formation is critical for changing unwanted habits because it highlights the importance of breaking the association between the trigger and the behavior. Individuals can disrupt the learned association and weaken the habitual response by changing the context or exposure to the trigger.

In conclusion, conditioning plays a critical role in forming habits, with repeated exposure to a particular trigger leading to automatic and unconscious responses. Understanding the mechanisms of conditioning provides insights into the potential for positive change and underscores the importance of disrupting learned associations to weaken unwanted habits.

The Role of Genetics in Habits

Genetics is thought to play a role in the development of habits, and there is evidence to suggest that certain genetic factors may contribute to the formation and maintenance of habitual behavior. One study by Beirut and colleagues (2010)[17] investigated the role of genetics in smoking behavior. They found that individuals with a particular genetic variant were more likely to have developed a habitual smoking pattern than those without the variant. Other research has suggested that genetic factors may also influence the tendency to engage in other habitual behaviors, such as overeating or substance use.

However, the extent to which genetics contributes to the development of habits is still a matter of debate. While some studies have identified specific genetic variants associated with habitual behavior, other research has found that environmental factors may play a more significant role in habit formation.

In a study by Huppertz and colleagues (2015)[18], the researchers investigated the influence of shared environmental factors on exercise behavior in children from age 7 to 12 years. The researchers analyzed data from a large sample of twins and their families. They found that shared environmental factors, such as the availability of exercise equipment in the home, significantly impacted exercise behavior. However, the influence of shared environmental factors decreased over time, indicating that genetics may become a more important factor in exercise behavior as children grow older.

The study highlights the complex interplay between genetics and environmental factors in shaping exercise behavior. While environmental factors such as access to exercise equipment and family members' social support can significantly impact exercise behavior, the role of genetics cannot be ignored. The findings suggest that interventions aimed at promoting exercise behavior should consider both genetic and environmental factors and that interventions may need to be tailored to different age groups to be most effective.

Overall, while genetics may play a role in forming and maintaining habits, the exact extent of its influence is still not fully understood. Future research may help clarify the complex interplay between genetic and environmental factors in developing habitual behaviors.

CHAPTER SUMMARY

Repetition is one of the most critical factors in habit formation, as repeated behavior becomes more automatic and habitual over time.

The Habit Cycle (Figure 1) is described as a four-step process. The first step is the trigger, followed by craving, action, and reward. Identifying triggers is essential in changing habits because it allows individuals to recognize the cues that prompt unwanted behavior and develop strategies to avoid or cope with them. Cravings are the psychological response to the trigger and create a sense of anticipation and desire for the habit to be enacted. Actions are the observable manifestation of the habit. Finally, the reward is the positive outcome that reinforces the habit cycle.

Habits are formed through a process of reinforcement learning in the brain that involves the formation of neural pathways that connect cues, cravings, actions, and rewards. Conditioning plays a critical role in forming habits, with repeated exposure to a particular trigger leading to automatic and unconscious responses. Genetics is thought to play a role in the development of habits, with some studies identifying specific genetic variants associated with habitual behavior.

Chapter 2: Why we do what we do?

"Watch your thoughts; they become your words. Watch your words; they become your actions. Watch your actions; they become your habits. Watch your habits; they become your character. Watch your character; it becomes your destiny." — Lao

Understanding why we do what we do is crucial in developing healthier habits. There are many factors that influence our behavior, including our environment, emotions, social norms, and personal values.

One theory that explains why we do what we do is the *Self-Determination Theory (SDT). SDT proposes that humans have three innate psychological needs: autonomy, competence, and relatedness* (Ryan & Deci, 2017)[19]. *Autonomy* refers to the need to feel in control of our own lives and decisions, while *competence* refers to the need to feel effective and capable. *Relatedness* refers to the need to feel connected to others and belong to a community.

Another theory that explains why we do what we do is the *Theory of Planned Behavior (TPB).* TPB suggests that our behavior is influenced by our beliefs about the consequences of our actions and the opinions of others (Ajzen, 1991)[20]. According to TPB, our behavior is determined by our attitudes towards the behavior, our subjective norms (perceived social pressure to engage in the behavior), and our perceived behavioral control (perceived ease or difficulty of performing the behavior).

Additionally, research has shown that our emotions and the reward systems in our brains influence our habits. The neurotransmitter dopamine plays a key role in habit formation by reinforcing the behavior through the pleasure or reward it provides (Everitt & Robbins, 2005)[21]. Therefore, habits can be seen as a way to regulate emotions and seek pleasure.

Understanding the underlying motivations and influences behind our behavior can help us identify and change unhealthy habits. By addressing the root causes of our habits, we can develop strategies to replace them with healthier behaviors that align with our values and goals.

The Unconscious Mind

The role of the unconscious mind in why we do what we do is a topic of great interest in psychology and neuroscience. The article by Bargh and Morsella (2008)[22] discusses the concept of the unconscious mind and its role in shaping our behavior, including habit formation. The authors argue that many of our daily behaviors are driven by automatic, unconscious processes that are influenced by our past experiences, social norms, and environmental cues. These automated processes operate without our conscious awareness, making them difficult to control or change.

Habits are formed through the repetition of actions over time, which leads to the formation of automatic, unconscious processes that guide our behavior. Once a habit is formed, it becomes difficult to change because it is deeply ingrained in our unconscious mind. Effective habit-change strategies need to take into account the automatic, unconscious processes that underlie our behavior and may require intentional effort and repetition to create new, more positive habits.

These unconscious processes are mediated by neural networks in the brain, which become activated in response to specific stimuli. The two main structures, the basal ganglia, and the amygdala, play a crucial role in forming habits and decision-making. The **basal ganglia**, for example, have been implicated in forming and maintaining habits, while the **amygdala** is involved in emotional processing and decision-making[23].

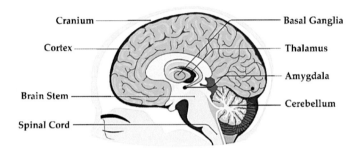

Figure 2. Structure of Brain

Basal Ganglia

The basal ganglia play a crucial role in habit formation and motor control. Here's how they contribute:

Habit Formation: The basal ganglia are involved in learning and automating repetitive behaviors. When we repeat actions over time, the basal ganglia help encode these behaviors into habits. For instance, think of brushing your teeth or tying your shoelaces – these actions become automatic due to the basal ganglia's influence.

Reward Processing: The basal ganglia receive input related to rewards and reinforcement. When we engage in a behavior that leads to a positive outcome (like enjoying a delicious meal), the basal ganglia reinforce that behavior, making it more likely to recur.

Motor Control: Beyond habits, the basal ganglia regulate voluntary movements. They fine-tune motor commands, ensuring smooth execution of actions like walking, reaching, and dancing.

Amygdala

The amygdala, on the other hand, is a key player in emotional processing and decision-making:

Emotional Significance: The amygdala processes emotional stimuli. It helps us recognize fear, pleasure, and other emotions. When you encounter something exciting or threatening, the amygdala lights up!

Decision-Making: The amygdala influences our decisions by evaluating emotional significance. It considers both positive and negative emotions when we choose between options. For example, when deciding whether to take a risk, the amygdala weighs potential rewards against potential dangers.

Memory Formation: The amygdala also contributes to memory consolidation, especially for emotionally charged events. Ever notice how vividly you remember intense experiences? The amygdala plays a role there.

Understanding the neurobiological basis of habit learning can have implications for treating various disorders involving habitual behaviors, such as addiction.

Recent research has also highlighted the importance of the *default mode network* (DMN) in shaping our behavior. The

DMN is a network of brain regions that become active when the mind is at rest and not focused on the external environment. It is thought to play a crucial role in self-referential processing, social cognition, and mental time travel, which may contribute to our ability to anticipate and plan for the future[24, 25]. DMN is said to be involved in constructing mental simulations of future events and that this ability is crucial for planning and decision-making. *Habits are formed through the repeated activation of specific brain circuits during the execution of behavior, forming a "habit loop"*[25]. The DMN may play a role in this process by allowing individuals to mentally simulate the desired behavior and its consequences, strengthening the connection between the relevant brain circuits.

Furthermore, the DMN may also be involved in the automatic activation of habits in response to environmental cues. This is because the *DMN is more active when individuals are in a passive, stimulus-driven state and less active during goal-directed behavior.* This suggests that when habits are formed, they become automatic and require less conscious effort to execute, as they are processed by the more automatic, default mode of brain function. DMN plays an important role in both the formation and execution of habits and suggests that this network may be a promising target for interventions to modify habitual behavior.

Despite its important role in shaping behavior, the unconscious mind remains largely inaccessible to conscious awareness. Nevertheless, researchers have developed a variety of techniques, such as neuroimaging and behavioral experiments, to study the neural and cognitive mechanisms underlying unconscious processes. These techniques have provided valuable insights into the ways in which the unconscious mind shapes our behavior and may ultimately lead to the development of more effective interventions for changing unwanted habits or behaviors.

The Impact of Childhood Experiences

Childhood experiences can have a profound impact on why we do what we do. Adverse experiences, such as abuse, neglect, or trauma, can lead to changes in brain structure and function and alterations in the stress response system. These changes can affect behavior, emotional regulation, and cognitive processes throughout the lifespan[26].

Childhood adversity can disrupt the development of self-regulatory skills, which are critical for forming healthy habits. Children who experience chronic or severe adversity may struggle with impulse control and have difficulty managing their emotions, making it challenging to establish and maintain healthy habits[26].

Studies have shown that childhood experiences can impact the development of neural circuits involved in decision-making, emotion regulation, and social behavior[27,28]. For example, early life stress has been linked to alterations in the amygdala, prefrontal cortex, and hippocampus, which may increase the risk for anxiety, depression, and addiction.

Moreover, childhood experiences can shape our beliefs and attitudes about ourselves, others, and the world around us. For instance, a child who grows up in an environment where they are consistently criticized or neglected may develop a negative self-concept, which may, in turn, influence their behavior and interpersonal relationships in adulthood.

Despite the potential long-term consequences of adverse childhood experiences, research has also shown that positive experiences, such as nurturing and supportive caregiving, can have protective effects and promote resilience[29]. Early intervention and support for children who have experienced adversity may therefore be crucial for promoting healthy development and preventing negative outcomes later in life.

Emotional Triggers

Emotions play a crucial role in the choices we make and the habits we form. Emotional triggers can activate the habit loop by creating a powerful urge or craving that prompts us to take action. For example, stress can trigger the habit of overeating or smoking. Research has shown that emotional states can affect neural activity in brain regions involved in habit formation, such as the basal ganglia and prefrontal cortex[30]. This suggests that emotional triggers can influence the strength of habit formation and lead to automatic and repeated behavior. In addition, emotional regulation skills have been found to be important in breaking unwanted habits and forming new ones[31]. By recognizing and managing emotional triggers, individuals can take control of their habits and work towards developing healthier ones.

Emotional Intelligence and Self-Awareness

Emotional intelligence (EI) and self-awareness are important factors in managing emotional triggers and breaking unwanted habits. EI refers to the ability to perceive, understand, and manage one's own emotions and the emotions of others. Self-awareness involves recognizing and understanding one's own emotions, thoughts, and behaviors. Research has shown that individuals with higher levels of EI and self-awareness are better able to regulate their emotions and resist emotional triggers that may lead to unwanted habits[32].

One study found that individuals who were more aware of their own emotional states were less likely to engage in impulsive behaviors, such as smoking and overeating[33]. Another study showed that individuals with higher levels of EI were better able to manage stress and cope with emotional triggers, leading to decreased incidence of unhealthy habits[34].

In addition, developing EI and self-awareness can also help individuals form healthier habits. By recognizing emotional triggers and understanding the underlying emotions that drive behavior, individuals can develop strategies to manage their emotions and make healthier choices[35].

Overall, the role of EI and self-awareness in managing emotional triggers and forming healthy habits is an important area of research that highlights the importance of emotional regulation skills in promoting overall health and well-being.

The Influence of Social Norm and Culture

Social norms and culture play an essential role in shaping our behavior and habits. Social norms refer to the unwritten rules of society that govern our behavior, such as how we dress, speak, and interact with others. Culture refers to the shared values, beliefs, customs, and traditions of a particular group or society. These factors can influence why we do what we do by providing us with a framework for appropriate behavior and expectations.

One example of how social norms can influence our behavior is the concept of "peer pressure." Adolescents and young adults may engage in certain behaviors, such as smoking or drinking because they want to fit in with their peers or meet social expectations. Similarly, cultural norms may dictate what types of foods we eat or how we celebrate holidays and events.

The Science of Habits

Social norms and culture can have a significant impact on our habits and behavior. Social norms are shaped by the culture we live in, and they influence our daily lives in subtle ways. For example, in some cultures, it is considered rude to talk loudly in public spaces, while in others, it is perfectly acceptable. These cultural differences can shape our habits and behavior, leading us to adopt certain practices and avoid others. Ultimately, our habits and behavior are influenced by the social norms and culture in which we live, and understanding these influences is critical to understanding ourselves and those around us.

In summary, social norms and culture can influence why we do what we do by shaping our behavior and expectations. It is important to be aware of these factors and how they may impact our habits and behavior. By understanding the influence of social norms and culture, we can make informed decisions about our behavior and strive to create habits that align with our values and goals.

CHAPTER SUMMARY

The Self-Determination Theory proposes that humans have three innate psychological needs: autonomy, competence, and relatedness. The Theory of Planned Behavior suggests that our beliefs about the consequences of our actions and the opinions of others influence our behavior. Our emotions and the reward systems in our brains also influence our habits. The basal ganglia and amygdala play a crucial role in forming habits and decision-making. Childhood experiences have a profound impact on why we do what we do, and emotional triggers can activate the habit loop. Emotional intelligence and self-awareness are important factors in managing emotional triggers and breaking unwanted habits. Social norms and culture play an essential role in shaping our behavior and habits and subtly influence our habits and behavior. Understanding these factors is critical to understanding ourselves and those around us and developing healthy habits.

Chapter 3: How to Change Habits?

"The only proper way to eliminate bad habits is to replace them with good ones." — Jerome Hines.

Habits are deeply ingrained patterns of behavior that are often difficult to change. However, changing habits is essential for personal growth and development. In this chapter, we will discuss evidence-based strategies for changing habits.

Changing habits can be challenging, but understanding the four-part cycle of habit formation can make it easier. By identifying and modifying the *trigger, craving, action,* and *reward* components, we can transform our habits for the better. This chapter will explore how to change habits by examining each part of the cycle and providing practical tips for making positive changes in our lives. With this knowledge, you can easily take control of your habits and achieve your goals.

Each part of the habit cycle - trigger, craving, action, and reward - plays a vital role in changing habits. Here's how:

Identify Triggers

The trigger, or cue, is the event or situation that prompts the habit. Triggers can be internal or external. Internal triggers may include emotions, physical sensations, or thoughts, while external triggers may include people, places, or situations. Once the trigger has been identified, developing a plan for avoiding or managing the trigger is essential. To change a habit, you must identify the trigger that sets it off. For example, if you have a habit of snacking when you're bored, the trigger might be feeling restless or having nothing to do. Once you've identified the trigger, you can create a plan to avoid or change it. For example, you could take a walk or read a book instead of snacking when you feel bored.

Define Craving

The craving is the desire or urge that follows the trigger. It's the feeling that motivates you to take action. To change a habit, you must replace the unhealthy craving with a healthier one. For example, if you have a habit of eating junk food when you feel stressed, you could replace that craving with the desire to exercise or meditate when you feel stressed.

Change Action

The action is the habit itself - the behavior that follows the trigger and craving. To change a habit, you need to replace the old action with a new one. For example, if you have a habit of smoking when you feel anxious, you could replace it with deep breathing exercises or going for a walk when you feel anxious.

Change Reward

The reward is the positive reinforcement that follows the action. It's the feeling of pleasure or satisfaction that you get from completing the habit. To change a habit, you need to find a new reward that provides the same positive reinforcement as the old one. For example, if you habitually drink sugary drinks when you feel thirsty, you could replace it with drinking water infused with fruit to still get the sweet taste and hydration.

By understanding and manipulating each part of the habit cycle, you can change the habit and create new, healthier habits. It takes time and effort, but it's possible to change any habit with persistence and the proper techniques.

Make a Plan

Changing habits requires a plan. This plan should include specific goals and strategies for achieving them. It may also involve enlisting the help of a friend, family member, or healthcare professional.

The Power of Mindfulness

Mindfulness is a powerful technique that can help individuals change their habits by increasing awareness of their thoughts, emotions, and behaviors. By being present and non-judgmental, mindfulness can help people recognize their habitual patterns and begin to make conscious choices to change them. Mindfulness has been found to be effective in reducing habit-related behaviors, such as smoking, overeating, and alcohol use[36]. In one study, mindfulness-based interventions were found to be more effective in reducing binge eating behaviors compared to traditional cognitive-behavioral therapy[37]. Another study found that mindfulness-based relapse prevention was effective in reducing the risk of relapse in individuals with substance use disorders[38]. These findings suggest that incorporating mindfulness practices into daily life can be a powerful tool for changing habits.

Replacing Old Habits with New Ones

Replacing old habits with new ones is a key strategy for changing habits. The process of replacing old habits with new ones involves identifying the old habit, understanding the triggers and rewards associated with it, and then creating a plan to replace the old habit with a new one. One practical approach is identifying a new behavior that satisfies the same underlying need as the old habit. For example, if the old habit is eating unhealthy snacks when feeling stressed, a new habit could be taking a brief walk or doing a relaxation exercise. It is also essential to make the new habit easy to do, such as keeping healthy snacks nearby or scheduling time for exercise. Research has shown that successfully replacing old habits with new ones requires patience and persistence, as it takes time for the brain to rewire itself. However, with practice and consistency, new habits can become automatic, leading to lasting behavior change.

One study conducted by Wood and Neal (2007)[3] examined the effectiveness of a habit replacement intervention to reduce snacking behaviors. The study found that participants who received the intervention were more successful in reducing their snacking behaviors than those who received only general information about healthy eating habits. The habit replacement intervention involved identifying triggers for snacking, identifying a substitute behavior that satisfied the same need, and practicing the new behavior until it became automatic. This study suggests that habit replacement can be an effective strategy for changing habits.

Identifying the habit to be changed

Identifying the habit that needs to be changed is an important step in the process of habit modification. According to Wood and Neal (2007)[3], identifying the specific behavior that needs to be modified is a critical first step in the process of habit change. It is important to understand the triggers that lead to the habit and its reward. This process can be aided by keeping a daily record of the behavior and any factors that may have influenced the behavior. By identifying the habits that need to be changed, it becomes possible to develop strategies to modify the behavior and create new habits. This may involve breaking the habit down into smaller components, such as reducing the frequency or duration of the behavior or replacing the behavior with a more desirable one. Identifying the habit to be changed is an important first step in the process of habit modification and can lead to successful long-term habit change (Wood & Neal, 2007)[3].

Creating a New Habit Cycle

Creating a new habit cycle involves identifying the behavior you want to change, determining the trigger for that behavior, and replacing the old behavior with a new one that provides a similar reward. This can be done through the use of cues, such as visual reminders or alarms, that signal the beginning of the new habit loop.

Use Positive Reinforcement

Positive reinforcement, such as rewarding yourself for sticking to the new habit, can also be effective in creating and maintaining the new habit loop. One study found that participants who received immediate positive reinforcement for a new behavior were more likely to continue the behavior than those who received delayed reinforcement or no reinforcement at all[39]. Another study showed that using specific cues, such as a specific time of day or a certain location, to trigger the new habit cycle effectively created and maintained the new habit[1].

Positive reinforcement involves rewarding yourself for making progress towards your goals. This can be as simple as giving yourself a pat on the back or treating yourself to a small indulgence.

Changing habits can be challenging, but it is possible with the right strategies and support. By identifying triggers, replacing old habits with new ones, making a plan, practicing mindfulness, and using positive reinforcement, anyone can successfully change their habits and achieve personal growth and development.

The Importance of Motivation and Will Power

The formation and maintenance of habits require motivation and willpower. Motivation is the driving force that compels individuals to initiate and sustain a behavior. At the same time, willpower is the ability to resist temptations and impulses that may interfere with the desired behavior. In the context of habit formation, motivation and willpower play a crucial role in creating and sustaining new habits and breaking old ones.

Research[19] has shown that motivation can be intrinsic or extrinsic. *Intrinsic motivation* arises from within oneself and is driven by personal interests, values, and beliefs, while *extrinsic motivation* is driven by external factors such as rewards, punishments, and social pressure. Intrinsic motivation is considered more effective in sustaining behavior change, as it is based on the individual's desires and values rather than external pressures.

Willpower, on the other hand, involves the ability to resist short-term temptations or impulses that may derail an individual's efforts to establish new habits. Research has demonstrated that *willpower is a finite resource that can be depleted over time through repeated acts of self-control, leading to a phenomenon known as "ego depletion."* Strategies such as creating positive affirmations, setting realistic goals, and engaging in activities that replenish willpower, such as exercise and adequate sleep, can help individuals maintain their willpower and avoid ego depletion.

Table 3.1: *Difference between intrinsic and extrinsic willpower*

Category	Definition	Examples
Intrinsic Willpower	The internal motivation or drive to pursue a task or goal for personal satisfaction or enjoyment.	A person who exercises regularly because they enjoy the activity or want to improve their health and well-being.
Extrinsic Willpower	The external motivation or drive to pursue a task or goal for a reward or to avoid punishment.	A student who studies hard to earn good grades or avoid failing a class, rather than because they enjoy the subject matter.

Note: Examples are for illustration purposes only and may not be applicable to every situation.

In addition to motivation and willpower, habit formation relies on the concept of "*implementation intentions*," which involves specifying when, where, and how a desired behavior will be carried out[40]. By creating a specific plan for behavior change, individuals can increase the likelihood of success in creating and maintaining new habits.

In summary, motivation and willpower are essential components in forming and maintaining habits. Intrinsic motivation is considered more effective in sustaining behavior change, and willpower can be strengthened through various strategies such as positive affirmations and replenishing activities. Finally, creating specific implementation intentions can help individuals successfully establish new habits.

Building Will Power

Willpower, or self-control, is the ability to resist immediate impulses and delay gratification for long-term goals. It is a crucial component in the formation and maintenance of healthy habits. Many studies have shown that individuals with high levels of willpower are more likely to achieve their goals and have better overall well-being. Building willpower can be challenging, but it is possible with consistent practice and commitment.

One effective way to build willpower is through regular practice of self-control tasks. Studies have shown that practicing self-control tasks, such as resisting tempting foods or refraining from checking social media, can increase overall self-control and willpower[41]. Another way to build willpower is through exercise. Research has shown that exercise can increase self-control and lead to better willpower[42]. Additionally, improving sleep quality and quantity can also enhance willpower. Studies have shown that sleep-deprived individuals have lower levels of self-control and willpower[43].

Meditation is another effective technique for building willpower. Research has shown that regular mindfulness meditation improves self-control and leads to better decision-making[35]. *Mindfulness meditation* involves focusing one's attention on the present moment and accepting thoughts and emotions without judgment. This practice can help individuals develop better awareness and control of their thoughts and impulses. Coloring a mandala is a form of mindfulness meditation that involves knowing the different aspects of mandala design and color choices. You are focused on the color combination and symmetrical nature of the mandala. Here is a good mindfulness mandala coloring book (*Mindfulness Mandala Coloring Meditation For Stress Reduction: Coloring Book for Adults for Stress Reduction*) for you to try.

Positive self-talk is also a powerful tool for building willpower. By changing negative self-talk into positive self-talk, individuals can improve their confidence and motivation.

Research has shown that individuals who engage in positive self-talk have better self-control and are more likely to achieve their goals[44].

In conclusion, building willpower is an essential component in developing healthy habits and achieving long-term goals. Consistent practice of self-control tasks, exercise, improving sleep quality and quantity, meditation, and positive self-talk are all effective ways to build willpower. It is important to note that building willpower takes time and commitment, but with regular practice, it is possible to strengthen and improve one's self-control.

Techniques to increase the likelihood of success.

There are several science-based techniques that can increase the likelihood of success in changing your habits.

Speak out your goals.

Self-affirmation and speaking one's goals out loud can be effective strategies in habit formation. When individuals engage in self-affirmation or verbalize their goals, they reinforce their personal values and beliefs, which can enhance motivation and self-control. This, in turn, can support developing and maintaining new habits.

Research conducted by Falk et al. (2015)[45] examined the impact of self-affirmation on behavior change. The study found that self-affirmation interventions led to positive changes in health-related behaviors, such as increasing physical activity and improving dietary choices. The authors suggested that self-affirmation helps individuals align their behavior with their desired self-image and values, making it easier to adopt new habits.

Speaking goals out loud can also be a powerful tool for habit formation. When individuals articulate their goals verbally, they create a sense of commitment and accountability. It helps reinforce their intentions and can serve as a reminder to engage in the desired behavior.

By combining self-affirmation and speaking goals out loud, individuals can enhance their commitment and motivation to form new habits. These practices can reinforce personal values, increase accountability, and create a sense of purpose and intention. Incorporating self-affirmation and vocalizing goals as part of habit-formation strategies can increase the likelihood of success.

Swap old habits with new ones.

Swapping an old habit with a new one is a strategy that can be effective in habit formation. By replacing an existing habit with a new, desired behavior, individuals can leverage the existing neural pathways and associations to establish and reinforce the new habit. This approach takes advantage of the brain's propensity for habit formation and allows for a smoother transition toward the desired behavior.

Research conducted by Lally et al. (2010)[1] supports the effectiveness of habit substitution in behavior change. The study examined the habit formation process and found that replacing an existing habit with a new behavior was associated with increased success in sustaining the desired behavior over time. The authors suggested that habit substitution can leverage the automaticity of existing habits and facilitate the formation of new habits by redirecting established cues and rewards.

Moreover, a study by Wood et al. (2012) investigated the effectiveness of *habit substitution* in promoting healthier dietary habits. The researchers found that participants who focused on substituting unhealthy snacks with more nutritious alternatives were more successful in reducing their overall calorie intake than those who solely relied on willpower to resist unhealthy snacks. This highlights the power of habit substitution as a practical approach to behavior change.

By consciously replacing an old habit with a new one, individuals can redirect their behavior towards the desired outcome. This process involves identifying the triggers and rewards associated with the old habit and finding alternative behaviors that can satisfy the same cues and provide similar rewards. The new habit can become more automatic and ingrained through repetition and consistency, leading to long-term behavior change.

Incorporating habit substitution into behavior change strategies can enhance the likelihood of success by leveraging the brain's existing neural pathways and associations. By swapping an old habit for a new one, individuals can tap into the power of habit formation and facilitate the adoption of healthier behaviors.

CHAPTER SUMMARY

This chapter provides evidence-based strategies for changing habits. The four-part cycle of habit formation - *trigger, craving, action,* and *reward* - is crucial in understanding how to change habits. Individuals can transform unhealthy habits into healthier ones by identifying and modifying each part of the cycle. The chapter discusses mindfulness, positive reinforcement, and habit substitution techniques. It also emphasizes the importance of motivation and willpower in forming and maintaining habits. Finally, the chapter suggests practical approaches to increasing the likelihood of success, including speaking out goals and swapping old habits with new ones.

Chapter 4: Overcoming Common Obstacles

"In the journey of habit-building, obstacles are not roadblocks; they are stepping stones. Embrace the challenges, for they sculpt your discipline and resilience. Remember, every small step forward is progress, even if it feels like a crawl."

Developing new habits is challenging and requires significant effort and consistency. Many people encounter obstacles in their pursuit of building new habits, such as lack of time, motivation, or self-discipline. However, understanding and addressing these obstacles can help individuals overcome them and successfully build new habits. One effective strategy is to break down the habit into small, manageable steps, which can help to reduce feelings of overwhelm and increase the likelihood of success. Additionally, positive reinforcement, such as rewarding oneself for progress made, can help maintain motivation and drive. Seeking social support from friends, family, or a support group can also provide accountability and encouragement. Finally, it is essential to identify and address any underlying emotional or psychological factors contributing to the obstacle, as these can significantly impact an individual's ability to build new habits.

One effective strategy is to break down the habit into small, manageable steps, which can help to reduce feelings of overwhelm and increase the likelihood of success.

Research has shown that developing habits is strongly influenced by an individual's environment and behavior. A study conducted by Lally et al.[1], found that, on average, it takes approximately 66 days for an individual to establish a new habit. However, this timeline can vary significantly depending on the individual and the habit being formed. The study also found that missing a day or two in the habit-building process did not significantly impact the overall success of forming the habit, but consistency over time was critical.

In addition to addressing obstacles, it is also important to understand the factors that can contribute to habit formation success. One essential factor is *self-awareness*, which involves being mindful of one's thoughts, emotions, and behaviors. This awareness can help individuals identify triggers that may lead to old habits and develop strategies to prevent or manage them. Additionally, setting specific, measurable, and attainable goals can help to provide clarity and direction in the habit-building process. This approach can help individuals establish a sense of achievement and build momentum toward their overall goals.

In conclusion, building new habits is a complex process that requires self-awareness, consistency, and the ability to overcome obstacles. Individuals can increase their chances of success in forming new habits by breaking down habits into manageable steps, using positive reinforcement, seeking social support, and addressing emotional and psychological factors. Understanding the science behind habit formation can also provide insight into the importance of consistency, self-awareness, and setting achievable goals, all of which can contribute to the successful establishment of new habits.

Procrastination

Procrastination is the act of delaying or postponing a task or action, often to the point of causing stress and anxiety. Procrastination is a common behavior that can interfere with productivity and success in various areas of life. The causes of procrastination can be attributed to a variety of factors, including perfectionism, lack of motivation, fear of failure, and lack of time management skills.

Perfectionism is often a major cause of procrastination. Individuals with perfectionistic tendencies tend to put off tasks until they can complete them perfectly, leading to unnecessary delays and missed deadlines. *Lack of motivation* is another common cause of procrastination. When individuals lack motivation, they may struggle to find the energy and drive needed to complete tasks, leading to procrastination.

Fear of failure is another common cause of procrastination. When individuals are afraid of failing or making mistakes, they may avoid tasks that could potentially lead to failure. This fear can lead to procrastination, as individuals put off tasks in an attempt to avoid the possibility of failure. Lastly, a *lack of time management* skills can also lead to procrastination. When individuals struggle with managing their time effectively, they may find themselves putting off tasks until the last minute, causing unnecessary stress and anxiety.

There are several strategies individuals can use to overcome procrastination.

Break tasks into smaller steps.

One effective strategy is to break tasks down into smaller, more manageable steps. By breaking down tasks, individuals can make the task seem less overwhelming and easier to complete. Let's say you have a large project to complete, but you keep procrastinating because the task seems overwhelming. Breaking the project into smaller steps can help make it feel more manageable and less intimidating. For example, instead of thinking about the entire project as a whole, you could break it down into smaller tasks like researching, outlining, drafting, and revising. Each of these smaller steps will feel more achievable and less daunting, making it easier to get started and stay motivated.

Set deadlines

Establishing deadlines for tasks creates a sense of urgency and helps to prioritize work. It can help individuals stay on track and avoid procrastination. An example of setting deadlines to overcome procrastination could be an individual who struggles to complete a project at work. Instead of waiting until the due date, they set specific deadlines for each section of the project to ensure that they are making progress and staying on track. This could involve breaking down the project into smaller tasks and assigning a deadline for each one, such as completing research by the end of the week or drafting the introduction by the end of the day. By setting deadlines, individuals can hold themselves accountable and avoid the temptation to procrastinate until the last minute.

Use a timer

Setting a timer for a specific amount of time can help with focus and concentration. The Pomodoro technique, for example, suggests working in 25-minute increments with 5-minute breaks in between.

The Pomodoro technique is a time management strategy that can help individuals overcome procrastination and improve productivity. It involves breaking down work into intervals of focused work and short breaks.

The technique is named after a tomato-shaped kitchen timer, the "Pomodoro," used by the technique's creator, Francesco Cirillo. The typical Pomodoro interval is 25 minutes of focused work, followed by a 5-minute break. After four Pomodoros, a longer break of 15-30 minutes is taken.

This technique helps to combat procrastination by providing a structured schedule for work and breaks. It can help individuals stay focused and motivated by providing them with regular breaks and achievable goals.

Research has shown that the Pomodoro technique can be effective in improving productivity and reducing procrastination. For example, a study published in the Journal of Business and Psychology found that the Pomodoro technique improved time management and work engagement among employees in an information technology company.

Overall, the Pomodoro technique can be useful for individuals who struggle with procrastination or difficulty staying focused. Breaking down work into manageable intervals and providing regular breaks can help individuals stay on task and accomplish their goals.

Remove distractions

Identify and remove distractions such as social media, email notifications, other interruptions, and closing unnecessary tabs on the internet browser that can hinder productivity.

Another example could be wearing noise-canceling headphones to eliminate external noise and distractions while working.

Create a conducive environment.

Creating a conducive environment is an effective strategy to overcome procrastination as it helps reduce distractions and create a positive work environment. When the environment is comfortable and distraction-free, it becomes easier to focus on the task at hand and stay motivated. For instance, if an individual is working on a project requiring concentration, they can create a work environment free from noise and interruptions. This can be done by finding a quiet room or using noise-cancelling headphones. Additionally, creating a comfortable work area with ergonomic furniture and adequate lighting can also enhance productivity and reduce the likelihood of procrastination. By creating a conducive environment, individuals can reduce the likelihood of being distracted and stay focused on their tasks, thereby reducing procrastination.

Get accountability

Accountability is the act of being responsible for something or someone, and it is one of the most effective strategies for overcoming procrastination. When we are accountable to someone, we are more likely to follow through on our commitments because we feel a sense of obligation to that person. This is because we don't want to disappoint them or let them down.

For example, if you are struggling to complete a project at work, you can make yourself accountable to your boss by setting a deadline and agreeing to update them on your progress. This creates a sense of responsibility and obligation to meet the deadline and keeps you on track.

Similarly, accountability can be created by sharing your goals with a friend, family member, or a professional coach. This can help you stay motivated and committed to your goals. By regularly checking in with your accountability partner and updating them on your progress, you are more likely to stay focused and on task.

Research has shown that accountability can significantly improve performance and increase the likelihood of achieving our goals. A study published in the Journal of Applied Psychology found that people who wrote down their goals shared them with someone else, and provided regular updates on their progress were 33% more successful in achieving their goals compared to those who did not have an accountability partner. Therefore, accountability can be a powerful tool to help overcome procrastination and achieve our goals.

Use positive self-talk

Positive self-talk is a technique that involves changing the internal dialogue and beliefs that a person has about themselves and their abilities. In the context of overcoming procrastination, positive self-talk can be used to combat negative thoughts and beliefs that may lead to self-doubt and procrastination. By intentionally replacing negative thoughts with positive affirmations, individuals can improve their confidence and self-efficacy, which can help them to take action and complete tasks more effectively.

For example, instead of saying to oneself, "I can't do this; it's too difficult," a person could use positive self-talk by saying, "I may find this challenging, but I have the skills and abilities to figure it out." By reframing the negative thought into a more positive one, individuals can overcome the feelings of being overwhelmed or having self-doubt that may be contributing to their procrastination.

Research has shown that positive self-talk can significantly reduce anxiety and increase task performance (Wood & colleagues, 2009)[44]. In addition, positive self-talk has been linked to improved overall well-being, self-esteem, and motivation.

Establish a routine or schedule.

Establishing a routine or schedule is a helpful strategy to overcome procrastination. When we establish a routine or schedule, we create a habit of doing certain tasks at certain times. This habit can be helpful in combating procrastination because we become accustomed to the idea of doing certain tasks at specific times. For example, if we set a routine of waking up early and doing our work first thing in the morning, we will be less likely to procrastinate because we have made a habit of doing work at that time. This also helps in reducing decision fatigue and increases efficiency. When we have a set schedule, we don't have to waste time and energy deciding what to do next, which can be a source of procrastination. By establishing a routine or schedule, we can train ourselves to become more disciplined and productive.

In conclusion, procrastination is a common behavior that can interfere with productivity and success in various areas of life. The causes of procrastination can be attributed to a variety of factors, including perfectionism, lack of motivation, fear of failure, and lack of time management skills. However, there are several strategies individuals can use to overcome procrastination, including breaking tasks down into smaller steps, establishing a routine or schedule, setting specific deadlines, establishing a system of rewards, and seeking support from others.

Distractions

Distractions are a common phenomenon that can significantly affect our productivity and well-being. There are various types of distractions, including external and internal distractions. *External distractions* are environmental factors that divert our attention away from the task at hand, such as noise, phone calls, or social media notifications. *Internal distractions*, on the other hand, are self-generated thoughts and emotions, such as anxiety or daydreaming, that impede our focus and concentration.

There are several techniques to avoid or minimize distractions. First, it is essential to identify the source of the distraction and take steps to remove or reduce it. For example, turning off notifications on your phone or working in a quiet space can help minimize external distractions. Additionally, using time management tools such as the Pomodoro technique, where you work for a set period and take short breaks, can help increase focus and minimize internal distractions.

Another technique for avoiding distractions is to establish a routine or schedule for completing tasks. This can help to create a sense of structure and focus, making it easier to prioritize tasks and minimize distractions. Additionally, prioritizing tasks can help to reduce the cognitive load of having multiple competing priorities, making it easier to focus on the most important tasks.

Positive self-talk is also a helpful technique for avoiding distractions. This involves replacing negative thoughts or self-talk with positive affirmations that promote focus and motivation. For example, instead of saying, "I'll never finish this task," you can say, "I can do this, and I will finish it." This technique can help to reduce anxiety and promote a positive mindset, which can help to minimize internal distractions.

In conclusion, distractions are common challenges that impede productivity and focus. Identifying the type of distraction and taking steps to remove or minimize it, establishing a routine or schedule, using positive self-talk, and using time management techniques can help to avoid distractions and increase focus. By adopting these strategies, we can enhance our productivity and overall well-being.

Dealing With Setbacks

Dealing with setbacks is an essential aspect of habit formation, as setbacks are inevitable in the process of building new habits. Common setbacks include lack of motivation, relapse into old habits, unexpected events, and external factors such as stress or illness.

Strategies for overcoming setbacks include identifying the cause of the setback, reframing negative self-talk, setting realistic goals, and seeking social support. A study by Hagger and colleagues (2010)[46] showed that individuals who used a self-regulatory strategy called "*implementation intentions*" were more likely to overcome setbacks and persist with their goals. This strategy involves making specific plans for how to deal with obstacles that may arise in pursuing a goal. Additionally, seeking social support from friends, family, or a therapist can be beneficial in providing encouragement, accountability, and guidance during setbacks. Overall, setbacks can be discouraging, but with the right strategies, they can be overcome, and progress toward building new habits can be maintained.

CHAPTER SUMMARY

The chapter begins with an overview of the challenges of developing new habits and the obstacles that can hinder the habit-building process, such as lack of time, motivation, or self-discipline. The chapter then presents effective strategies for overcoming these obstacles, such as *breaking down habits into manageable steps*, using *positive reinforcement*, *seeking social support*, and *addressing emotional and psychological factors*. The chapter also explores the causes of procrastination and strategies for overcoming it, such as *breaking tasks into smaller steps, setting deadlines, using a timer*, and *removing distractions*. The chapter also discusses various types of distractions and techniques for avoiding or minimizing them. Finally, the chapter addresses setbacks in the habit-forming process. It provides strategies for overcoming setbacks, such as identifying the cause of setbacks, reframing negative self-talk, setting realistic goals, and seeking social support.

Chapter 5: Most common bad habits

"Breaking bad habits is like unshackling yourself from self-imposed chains. Each small victory is a link you've shattered, paving the way to freedom. Remember, you're not defined by your past habits; you're sculpting a better future."

There are many bad habits that people may want to break, but some of the most common ones include:

1. Smoking
2. Overeating/overeating unhealthy foods
3. Nail biting
4. Procrastination
5. Excessive alcohol consumption
6. Excessive social media or screen time

It is important to note that everyone may have different bad habits that they want to break, and what may be a bad habit for one person may not be for another. This chapter will explore the habit cycle – Trigger, Craving, Action, Reward (TCAR) associated with each bad habit and explore options to break these bad habits.

Habit Cycle (TCAR steps)

How to Stop Smoking? (using TCAR)

Smoking is a harmful habit that is not only detrimental to one's health but also has significant negative effects on the environment. Quitting smoking can be challenging due to the addictive nature of nicotine. However, breaking the habit can improve overall health and well-being. One effective way to quit smoking is by understanding and changing the habit cycle. The habit cycle consists of four steps: Trigger, Craving, Action, and Reward (TCAR).

The first step is the trigger. Triggers can be internal or external factors that initiate the smoking habit. Examples of external triggers include social situations, stress, or seeing someone else smoke. Internal triggers may consist of boredom, anxiety, or craving a cigarette after a meal. It is important to identify the triggers that lead to smoking and try to avoid or manage them effectively.

The second step is the craving. Cravings are the intense desire to smoke a cigarette triggered by the identified trigger. Nicotine addiction can cause these cravings, and they can be challenging to resist. To overcome cravings, it is essential to develop coping mechanisms, such as deep breathing, exercise, or meditation, that can help manage the cravings.

The third step is the action. This step refers to the act of smoking a cigarette. Breaking this step requires an effort to substitute smoking with healthy activities. For instance, instead of smoking during a break, an individual can take a walk, read a book, or listen to music.

The fourth step is the reward. This step refers to the positive outcome of smoking, such as stress relief or social interaction. To stop smoking, it is essential to find alternative ways of getting the reward. For instance, an individual can join a support group, engage in stress-reducing activities, or spend time with friends who do not smoke.

The Three-Step process of breaking bad habits can help you :

STEP 1. DEFINE THE CURRENT HABIT CYCLE

Recognize the situations, people, or emotions that make you want to smoke. What cravings prompt you to take the action? What reward do you receive? For people with a habit of smoking:

Trigger: This is the cue or context that prompts the smoker to smoke. Triggers can differ for each person, but common triggers include stress, boredom, social situations, and certain times of day.

Craving: After the trigger, the smoker experiences a craving or urge to smoke. This can be both physical and psychological, as nicotine is addictive, and smoking may be associated with certain emotions or activities.

Action: The smoker then performs the action of smoking a cigarette, often in a habitual and automatic manner.

Reward: The act of smoking provides a reward or positive reinforcement for the smoker, which can include feelings of relaxation, pleasure, or relief from withdrawal symptoms.

STEP 2. CREATE AN ALTERNATE HABIT CYCLE

Develop an alternate habit cycle. Make the trigger less noticeable, reduce the appeal of the craving, make the smoking action more challenging to perform, and make the reward for not smoking more desirable. You do not have to make changes in all four steps. You just need to break the cycle to pick the most feasible step.

An example of an alternate habit cycle includes:

The Science of Habits

Trigger: After a meal

Craving: The craving for a cigarette arises

Action: *Instead of lighting a cigarette, the person goes for a walk or does a deep breathing exercise.*

Reward: The person feels a sense of accomplishment and satisfaction from breaking the habit and engaging in a healthy alternative. Additionally, they may experience improved breathing and a sense of relaxation from the exercise or deep breathing.

Over time, this new habit cycle can become automatic and replace the old habit of smoking after a meal.

Another example of an alternate habit cycle:

Trigger: After finishing a meal

Craving: The desire for a satisfying taste in the mouth

Action: *Chew a piece of gum or suck on a mint*

Reward: Fresh breath and a satisfying taste in the mouth without the harmful effects of smoking.

STEP 3: STAY MOTIVATED

Remind yourself of the reasons why you want to quit smoking, such as improving your health or saving money. Celebrate your successes along the way to stay motivated.

By following these steps and using the habit cycle model (trigger, craving, action, reward), individuals can successfully break their smoking habit and live healthier lives.

Studies have shown that a combination of behavioral and pharmacological interventions can be effective in quitting smoking. Some of the effective behavioral interventions include cognitive-behavioral therapy, support groups, and motivational interviewing. Pharmacological interventions include nicotine replacement therapy, such as patches, gum, and lozenges, and prescription medications like bupropion and varenicline.

In conclusion, quitting smoking can be challenging, but understanding and changing the habit cycle can make it easier. Identifying and managing triggers, coping with cravings, substituting smoking with healthy activities, and finding alternative rewards are effective strategies to quit smoking. Combining behavioral and pharmacological interventions can also increase the chances of successfully quitting smoking. It is never too late to quit smoking and start living a healthier life.

How to Stop Overeating Unhealthy Foods?

Overeating unhealthy foods can lead to various health problems such as obesity, heart disease, and type 2 diabetes. Breaking the habit of overeating unhealthy foods can be difficult, but it is achievable with the help of a 4 step habit cycle (Trigger, Craving, Action, and Reward) approach. This section will discuss evidence-based strategies to help you stop overeating unhealthy foods.

Trigger: Identify Your Triggers

The first step in breaking the habit of overeating unhealthy foods is identifying your triggers. Triggers are the events or situations that lead to your overeating. For example, you may overeat when stressed, bored, or watching TV. By identifying your triggers, you can become more aware of when you are likely to overeat and take steps to avoid these situations or find healthier ways to cope with them.

Craving: Change Your Cravings

The second step in breaking the habit of overeating unhealthy foods is to change your cravings. Cravings are the intense desire for a specific type of food, such as chocolate or chips. One strategy to change your cravings is substituting unhealthy foods with healthier options. For example, try snacking on carrot sticks or apple slices instead of reaching for a bag of chips. Another strategy is to practice mindfulness and pay attention to your body's hunger and fullness signals.

Action: Change Your Actions

The third step in breaking the habit of overeating unhealthy foods is to change your actions. Actions are the behaviors you engage in when you overeat, such as grabbing a bag of chips or ordering a pizza. One strategy to change your actions is to make healthy choices easier. For example, stock your fridge and pantry with healthy foods so they are more easily accessible than unhealthy options. Another strategy is to practice portion control and use smaller plates to help you eat smaller portions.

Reward: **Reward Yourself**

The fourth and final step in breaking the habit of overeating unhealthy foods is to reward yourself. Rewards are the positive outcomes that reinforce your overeating behavior. Instead of rewarding yourself with unhealthy foods, try rewarding yourself with healthy options. For example, if you have successfully avoided overeating unhealthy foods for a week, treat yourself to a massage or a movie.

Breaking the habit of overeating unhealthy foods can be challenging, but with the help of a 4 step habit cycle approach, it is achievable. By identifying your triggers, changing your cravings actions, and rewarding yourself with healthy options, you can successfully break the habit of overeating unhealthy foods and achieve a healthier lifestyle.

The Three-Step process to break a bad habit of Overeating Unhealthy Food includes:

STEP 1. DEFINE THE CURRENT HABIT CYCLE

Here is an example of the current habit cycle for overeating unhealthy food:

Trigger: Feeling stressed or bored

Craving: A desire for comfort or distraction

Action: Eating unhealthy food

Reward: Temporary relief from negative emotions or boredom

The Science of Habits

This habit cycle can become reinforced over time, leading to unhealthy eating habits and negative health consequences. It is essential to recognize and understand this habit cycle to break it and develop healthier habits.

STEP 2. CREATE AN ALTERNATE HABIT CYCLE

Develop an alternate habit cycle. Make the trigger less noticeable, reduce the appeal of the craving, make the overeating action more challenging to perform, and make the reward for not overeating more desirable. You do not have to make changes in all four steps. You just need to break the cycle to pick the most feasible step.

Here's an example of an alternate habit cycle for stopping overeating unhealthy foods:

Trigger: Feeling hungry and craving a snack.

Craving: Wanting something sweet and satisfying.

Action: Instead of reaching for a bag of chips or cookies, choose a healthier alternative, such as a piece of fruit, a handful of nuts, or a low-calorie protein bar.

Reward: Feeling good about making a healthier choice and feeling satisfied with the protein-rich snack.

In this alternate habit cycle, the trigger and craving are the same as the original habit cycle, but the action and reward have been changed to promote healthier eating habits. By choosing a more nutritious snack option, the individual still satisfies their craving for something sweet while also feeling good about making a healthier choice. Over time, this new habit cycle can replace the old one and lead to healthier eating habits.

Another example of an alternate habit cycle for stopping overeating unhealthy foods:

Trigger: Feeling bored or stressed after a long day at work.

Craving: Wanting something sweet and satisfying.

Action: *Instead of reaching for junk food, take a quick break and do a short meditation or breathing exercise to calm down and relax. After the meditation or breathing exercise, prepare a healthy snack like a fruit salad or a vegetable plate.*

Reward: Enjoy the delicious and healthy snack while feeling proud and accomplished for making a good choice that supports overall health and well-being.

This habit cycle is another example of how to replace overeating unhealthy food with a healthier alternative. The trigger is feeling bored or stressed after a long day at work. The craving is to calm down and relax. Instead of reaching for junk food, take a quick break and do a short meditation or breathing exercise. This helps to calm the mind and reduce stress levels. After the meditation or breathing exercise, the action is to prepare a healthy snack like a fruit salad or a vegetable plate. The reward is enjoying the delicious and nutritious snack while feeling proud and accomplished for making a good choice that supports overall health and well-being. This habit cycle creates a new habit of choosing healthy snacks and calming techniques to deal with stress rather than reaching for unhealthy junk food.

STEP 3: STAY MOTIVATED

To stay motivated with an alternate habit loop for stopping overeating unhealthy food habit, there are a few strategies that can be helpful:

Set specific and achievable goals: Instead of just saying, "I want to stop overeating unhealthy foods," set specific and achievable goals for yourself. For example, you could set a goal to eat a certain number of servings of fruits and vegetables daily or cook at home at least three times a week.

Use positive self-talk: When you crave unhealthy foods, use positive self-talk to remind yourself of your goals and the benefits of making healthier choices. For example, you might say, "I am choosing to nourish my body with healthy foods that make me feel good."

Surround yourself with support: Surround yourself with supportive friends and family members who encourage your healthy habits. You can also join a support group or find an accountability partner to help keep you motivated.

Celebrate your successes: When you make progress toward your goals, take time to celebrate your accomplishments. This can help you stay motivated and build momentum for making more positive changes in the future.

Using these strategies, you can stay motivated and committed to your alternate habit cycle to stop overeating unhealthy food habits. *Remember that changing habits takes time and effort, but it is possible to make lasting changes for better health and well-being with persistence and support.*

How to Stop Nail Biting?

Nail biting, also known as onychophagia, is a common habit that can cause damage to nails and skin around the nails and increase the risk of infections. It is estimated that about 20-30% of the general population bites their nails, with a higher prevalence among children and adolescents[47].

Breaking the habit of nail biting can be challenging, as it often happens unconsciously and can be triggered by different factors such as stress, boredom, or anxiety. Understanding the habit loop and developing new habits can be effective strategies for stopping nail biting.

Trigger: Identify Your Triggers

Identifying the triggers for nail biting is the first step in changing the habit cycle. Triggers can be physical, such as rough or uneven nails, or emotional, such as stress or boredom. Identifying the triggers makes it easier to recognize when the urge to bite the nails is likely to occur.

Craving: Understand Your Craving

The craving phase is characterized by a feeling of tension or discomfort that arises after the trigger. In the case of nail-biting, the craving may be driven by a need to release stress or anxiety. Recognizing the craving and finding alternatives to satisfy the need for tension release is key to breaking the habit.

Action: Identify Your Action

The action phase involves the actual behavior of nail biting. It is important to replace this behavior with a new habit that satisfies the craving in a healthy way. One option is to use a stress ball or fidget toy to release tension instead of biting the nails. Another option is to use a bitter-tasting nail polish or bandage to cover the nails and discourage biting.

Reward: Define Your Reward

In the reward phase, the brain associates the behavior with a positive outcome, reinforcing the habit cycle. It is vital to find a healthy and positive reward for resisting the urge to bite the nails, such as giving oneself a compliment or engaging in a favorite activity. Over time, the brain will learn to associate the new habit with a positive outcome, making it easier to resist the urge to bite the nails.

In addition to these steps, it is important to practice good nail care, such as trimming and filing the nails regularly to prevent rough edges. Seeking support from friends, family, or a healthcare professional can also help break the habit of nail biting.

In conclusion, breaking the habit of nail-biting requires identifying the triggers, finding alternatives to satisfy the craving, replacing the behavior with a new habit, and rewarding oneself for success. With time and effort, it is possible to stop nail biting and maintain healthy nails and skin.

The Three-Step process to stopping nail biting habit includes:

STEP 1. DEFINE THE CURRENT HABIT CYCLE

Here is an example of one's current habit cycle:

Trigger: The trigger for nail biting can be different for each person, but it is usually a feeling of stress, anxiety, boredom, or nervousness. It can also be a habit that has been formed over time.

Craving: The craving is the desire to bite the nails to relieve stress or anxiety, or simply out of habit. It can feel satisfying or calming in the moment.

Action: The action is the actual biting of the nails. It may involve biting them down to the skin or using the teeth to tear off pieces of the nails.

Reward: The reward for nail biting is the temporary relief of stress or anxiety or the feeling of satisfaction that comes from completing the habit. However, in the long term, the habit can cause physical damage to the nails and cuticles, leading to pain and even infection.

This habit cycle can become deeply ingrained, making it difficult to break the habit. However, with determination and the right approach, it is possible to overcome nail biting and develop healthier habits.

STEP 2. CREATE AN ALTERNATE HABIT CYCLE

Develop an alternate habit cycle. Make the trigger less noticeable, reduce the appeal of the craving, make the nail-biting action more challenging to perform, and make the reward for not biting nails more desirable. You do not have to make changes in all four steps. You just need to break the cycle to pick the most feasible step.

Here's an example of an alternate habit cycle for stopping nail biting:

Trigger: Feeling bored, stressed, or anxious.

Craving: Getting the urge to bite nails.

Action: Instead of biting nails, chewing gum, or chewing a toy to keep the mouth busy, or play with fidget toys. Start chewing it instead of biting your nails.

Reward: Over time, the reward will be having longer and healthier nails and the satisfaction of breaking the habit. Additionally, it can help to reward yourself with something you enjoy, like a new book or a nice dinner, for every week or month that you avoid nail biting.

STEP 3: STAY MOTIVATED

Staying motivated with the alternate habit cycle for stopping nail biting involves some key strategies.

Firstly, it is crucial to track progress and celebrate even small successes. This can help to build momentum and maintain motivation over time. For instance, one can use a habit-tracking app or a journal to record each day that they avoid nail-biting and acknowledge the progress made.

Secondly, finding support from friends, family or a support group can be beneficial in maintaining motivation. Encouragement and positive reinforcement from others can provide a sense of accountability and make staying committed to the new habit cycle easier.

Thirdly, finding alternative stress-relief techniques can help to reduce the likelihood of reverting to the old habit. Engaging in activities like deep breathing, stretching, or exercise can provide a healthy outlet for stress and anxiety, reducing the temptation to nail biting.

Finally, practicing self-compassion and acknowledging that slip-ups may occur can help to avoid feeling discouraged or defeated. Rather than beating oneself up for a setback, viewing it as a learning opportunity and refocusing on the alternate habit cycle to continue making progress is essential.

How to Stop Procrastination at Work?

Procrastination is a common problem that affects many people in their daily lives. It can lead to stress, anxiety, and poor performance at work or school. However, overcoming procrastination can be challenging, and many struggle to break the habit. This section will explore evidence-based strategies to help individuals stop procrastinating and become more productive at work.

Trigger: **Identify Your Triggers**

Procrastination often begins with a trigger, such as feeling overwhelmed, anxious, or bored. Recognizing these triggers is the first step to overcoming procrastination. Common triggers include large or complex tasks, fear of failure, lack of interest or motivation, and distractions like social media or emails.

Craving: **Understand Your Cravings**

The craving associated with procrastination is often the desire to avoid the task at hand and do something more enjoyable or easier. This can lead to negative emotions such as guilt, shame, and anxiety.

Action: **Identify Action**

To overcome procrastination, individuals need to act. One effective strategy is to break tasks down into smaller, more manageable steps. This helps to reduce feelings of overwhelm and increase motivation. Setting specific, achievable goals and creating a schedule or timeline can help individuals stay on track and avoid distractions.

Reward: **Define Your Reward**

The reward for overcoming procrastination is the sense of accomplishment and reduced stress. Celebrating small victories along the way can help individuals stay motivated and focused. This can include taking breaks, rewarding oneself with something enjoyable, or seeking support from friends or colleagues.

The Three-Step process to stopping nail biting habit includes:

STEP 1. DEFINE THE CURRENT HABIT CYCLE

Here's an example of the habit cycle for procrastination:

Trigger: A task or responsibility that needs to be done, such as a work project or household chore.

Craving: The desire to avoid the task due to feelings of anxiety, boredom, or overwhelm.

Action: Engaging in a distracting activity instead of starting or completing the task, such as scrolling through social media or watching TV.

Reward: The temporary relief from negative feelings and the short-term pleasure of the distracting activity reinforces the habit of procrastination. However, the long-term consequences of not completing the task can lead to increased stress and anxiety.

The current habit cycle for procrastination typically involves a trigger, which could be anything from a looming deadline to a difficult task that requires significant effort or skill. This trigger creates a sense of anxiety or stress, leading to a craving for a way to avoid or escape the task at hand. The action taken in response to this craving is often procrastination itself, such as scrolling through social media, watching TV, or engaging in other distractions that offer temporary relief from the stress of the trigger. The reward of procrastination is the temporary relief from stress, reinforcing the behavior and making it more likely to be repeated in the future. Over time, this habit cycle becomes automatic and can be difficult to break without intentional effort and strategies for change.

STEP 2. CREATE AN ALTERNATE HABIT CYCLE

Make the trigger less noticeable, reduce the appeal of the craving, make the procrastination action more challenging to perform, and make the reward for not procrastinating more desirable. You do not have to make changes in all four steps. You just need to break the cycle to pick the most feasible step.

Here's an example of an alternate habit cycle for stopping procrastination at work:

Trigger: Feeling overwhelmed by a task or project.

Craving: The desire to avoid the task due to feelings of anxiety, boredom, or overwhelm.

Action: Instead of avoiding the task, break it down into smaller, manageable steps. Take the first step, no matter how small it may be, and set a specific time frame for completing it.

Reward: Celebrate the completion of each step with a small reward, such as a short break to do something enjoyable or a favorite snack.

Over time, the sense of accomplishment and progress towards completing the task will serve as a powerful motivator to continue taking action and making progress, ultimately leading to the successful completion of the project or task.

STEP 3: STAY MOTIVATED

Staying motivated with the alternate habit cycle of stopping procrastination involves several strategies. First, it is essential to recognize and celebrate any progress made toward the new habit, even if it is small. This can help build momentum and confidence in the ability to change habits. Another helpful strategy is to visualize the benefits of breaking the habit, such as increased productivity, reduced stress, and a sense of accomplishment. This can help keep the motivation strong and remind the individual of the positive outcomes they are working towards.

Additionally, having an accountability partner or support system can provide encouragement and help maintain motivation. Regularly checking in with this individual or group can help the individual stay on track and motivated to continue the new habit loop. Finally, it is essential to recognize that setbacks are a normal part of the process and not to let them derail progress. Instead, the individual can recommit to the new habit cycle and continue progressing toward their goal.

How to Stop Drinking Alcohol?

Alcohol consumption can be a serious issue for some people, leading to addiction and negative health consequences. It's important to address the habit loop associated with drinking to break the cycle and make positive changes. This section will provide evidence-based strategies for breaking the habit cycle and stopping alcohol consumption.

Trigger: **Identify Triggers and Avoid Them**

One of the first steps in breaking the habit cycle of alcohol consumption is to identify the triggers that lead to drinking. Common triggers include stress, social situations, and negative emotions. Once you have identified your triggers, it's essential to develop strategies to avoid them or cope with them in a healthy way. For example, if social situations are a trigger for you, you can try attending events that don't involve alcohol or limiting your time at events that do.

Craving: **Develop New Habits to Manage Cravings**

Cravings can be a powerful force in the habit cycle of alcohol consumption. To manage cravings, developing new habits that provide a similar reward or feeling of satisfaction is essential. Exercise, meditation, and spending time with loved ones are all healthy habits that can help manage cravings. Having a support system, whether through friends, family, or a professional counselor, is essential.

Action: **Make a Plan and Stick to It**

Breaking the habit cycle of alcohol consumption requires a plan and commitment to follow through. Set realistic goals for reducing or eliminating alcohol consumption and create a plan to achieve those goals. This may include seeking professional help, attending support groups, or finding healthy activities to replace drinking. Staying committed to the plan is essential, even when faced with challenges or setbacks.

Reward: Celebrate Milestones and Successes

Breaking the habit cycle of alcohol consumption is a significant achievement, and it's important to celebrate milestones and successes along the way. This can provide a sense of accomplishment and motivation to continue making positive changes. Celebrate milestones by treating yourself to something you enjoy that doesn't involve alcohol, such as a massage, a movie, or a nice meal. Celebrate successes by sharing your accomplishments with your support system and reflecting on your positive changes.

Breaking the habit loop of alcohol consumption requires commitment and effort, but it is possible. By identifying triggers, developing new habits to manage cravings, making a plan and sticking to it, and celebrating successes along the way, you can break the cycle of alcohol addiction and live a healthier, happier life.

The three-step process to stopping alcohol consumption includes:

STEP 1. DEFINE THE CURRENT HABIT CYCLE

Here is an example of a current habit cycle for alcohol consumption:

Trigger: Social events, stress, or negative emotions.

Craving: Feeling the need to have a drink to feel relaxed or to cope with stress or negative emotions.

Action: Drinking alcohol, either alone or with others, to feel the desired effects of relaxation, pleasure, or escape.

Reward: Feeling temporarily relieved from stress or negative emotions, feeling more relaxed, or experiencing pleasure from the taste or effects of alcohol.

The current habit cycle for alcohol consumption starts with the trigger of stress, anxiety, or social situations. The craving involves the desire to relieve stress, socialize, or to feel the euphoric effects of alcohol. The action is the consumption of alcohol, which provides immediate relief and relaxation. The reward is the temporary reduction of stress or anxiety, the feeling of relaxation and euphoria, and the social acceptance and enjoyment that comes with drinking. Over time, this habit cycle can become deeply ingrained and automatic, making it difficult to quit or cut back on alcohol consumption.

STEP 2. CREATE AN ALTERNATE HABIT CYCLE

Make the trigger less noticeable, reduce the appeal of the craving, make the alcohol consumption action more challenging to perform, and make the reward for not drinking alcohol more desirable. You do not have to make changes in all four steps. You just need to break the cycle, so pick the most feasible step.

Here's an example of an alternate habit cycle for stopping alcohol consumption:

Trigger: Feeling stressed or overwhelmed after a long day at work.

Craving: Feeling the need to have a drink to feel relaxed or to cope with stress or negative emotions. *Instead of reaching for alcohol, take a few deep breaths and remind yourself of your reasons for wanting to quit, such as improved health, better relationships, or financial savings.*

Action: After taking a moment to pause and reflect, engage in a healthy and enjoyable activity that distracts you from the urge to drink, such as going for a walk, calling a friend, or working on a hobby.

Reward: Feel proud and accomplished for making a positive choice that supports your well-being and enjoy the benefits of engaging in a healthy and rewarding activity. Over time, the more you practice this alternate habit loop, the easier it will become to resist the urge to drink and replace it with healthier and more fulfilling behaviors.

STEP 3: STAY MOTIVATED

Staying motivated in stopping alcohol consumption can be challenging, but there are several ways to maintain the motivation to break the habit cycle. One effective way is to set achievable goals and track progress regularly. For example, setting a goal to reduce alcohol consumption by a certain percentage every week and keeping a record of the amount consumed can help people stay motivated. Another way is to find a support group or accountability partner who can provide encouragement and help you stay on track. It is also essential to focus on the positive outcomes of breaking the habit cycle, such as improved physical and mental health, better relationships, and increased productivity. Celebrating small successes can also help boost motivation and reinforce the new habit cycle. Additionally, engaging in healthy activities like exercise, meditation, or pursuing hobbies can serve as healthy alternatives to drinking and help maintain motivation.

How to Stop Excessive Screen Time?

Excessive screen time has become a prevalent problem today, with many people spending several hours each day on their electronic devices. Studies have shown that excessive screen time can lead to adverse health outcomes, including poor sleep, eye strain, and decreased physical activity. Breaking the habit of excessive screen time can be challenging, but it is possible by using the four-step habit cycle model.

Trigger: Identify Triggers and Avoid Them

The trigger for excessive screen time can vary from person to person, but it often stems from boredom, stress, or the need to escape from reality. Notifications, such as social media updates or messages from friends, can also trigger it.

Craving: Develop New Habits to Manage Cravings

The craving associated with excessive screen time is the desire for distraction, entertainment, or social connection. Many people find it difficult to resist the temptation to check their phones or browse social media when bored or stressed.

Action: Make a Plan and Stick to It

The action associated with excessive screen time is the act of picking up the device and using it for an extended period. This action can lead to a cycle of addiction, as the brain releases dopamine in response to the activity, creating a pleasurable sensation that reinforces the behavior.

Reward: Celebrate Milestones and Successes

The reward associated with excessive screen time is the temporary relief from boredom, stress, or the desire for social connection. However, this reward is short-lived and can lead to adverse health outcomes over time.

The Science of Habits

Breaking the habit cycle of excessive screen time requires commitment and effort, but it is possible. By identifying triggers, developing new habits to manage cravings, making a plan and sticking to it, and celebrating successes along the way, you can break the cycle of excessive screen time and live a healthier, happier life.

The three-step process to stopping alcohol consumption includes:

STEP 1. DEFINE THE CURRENT HABIT CYCLE

Here is an example of a current habit cycle for alcohol consumption:

Trigger: A person encounters a trigger such as boredom, stress, or a desire for entertainment.

Craving: The person experiences a craving to use electronic devices, such as smartphones, tablets, or computers, to distract themselves from the trigger and to seek pleasure or entertainment.

Action: The person takes action and uses electronic devices for an extended period of time, leading to excessive screen time use.

Reward: The person experiences a sense of pleasure, distraction, or entertainment as a reward for their screen time use, which reinforces the habit cycle and increases the likelihood of repeating the behavior.

STEP 2. CREATE AN ALTERNATE HABIT CYCLE

Make the trigger less noticeable, reduce the appeal of the craving, make the excessive screen time action more challenging to perform, and make the reward for not spending more time on screen more desirable. You do not have to make changes in all four steps. You just need to break the cycle, so pick the most feasible step.

Here's an example of an alternate habit cycle for stopping excessive screen time:

Trigger: If you are feeling bored, *find other ways to occupy your time, such as reading a book or walking.*

Craving: The person experiences a craving to use electronic devices, such as smartphones, tablets, or computers, to distract themselves from the trigger and to seek pleasure or entertainment. If the craving is for social connection, *reach out to a friend or family member in person or through a phone call.*

Action: *Instead of scrolling through social media, engage in a hobby like drawing or playing an instrument.*

Reward: *After engaging in a hobby or spending time with loved ones, take a moment to appreciate the sense of satisfaction and accomplishment that comes from pursuing meaningful activities.*

STEP 3: STAY MOTIVATED.

To stay motivated, it is important to set realistic goals and track progress over time. Celebrate small victories along the way, such as reducing screen time by a certain amount each day or finding new hobbies to replace the habit. Additionally, seek support from friends and family who can provide encouragement and accountability. Finally, be kind to yourself and recognize that breaking the habit of excessive screen time takes time and effort.

Chapter 6. How Long Does It Take to Form a Habit?

"Habits are the invisible architects of our lives. Each small choice, each repeated action, shapes our destiny. So, build habits that construct greatness—one brick at a time."

In the realm of habit formation, one question that often arises is: How long does it take to form a habit? The journey from consciously performing an action to becoming an automatic behavior can vary greatly depending on numerous factors. In this chapter, we will explore the concept of habit formation and delve into the research surrounding the timeline for habit development. By understanding the factors that influence habit formation, we can gain insights into effectively cultivating new habits and replacing old ones.

The Habit Formation Process

Before delving into the timeline, it's essential to understand the process of habit formation. Habits are formed through a repetitive cycle consisting of a trigger, craving, action, and a reward. This cycle is reinforced by the brain's neuroplasticity and the strengthening of neural pathways. As we repeat a behavior in response to a trigger and experience a reward, the habit becomes ingrained and automatic.

The Myth of the 21-Day Rule

One common belief is that it takes 21 days to form a habit. Dr. Maxwell Maltz, a plastic surgeon in the 1950s, noticed a peculiar trend among his patients. After performing surgeries like nose jobs, patients took approximately 21 days to adjust to their new appearance. The same could be observed when patients had limbs amputated, with patients detecting a phantom limb for 21 days before adapting. Dr. Maltz realized the 21-day cycle also applied to forming new habits based on his own experience of adopting new behaviors. This was his own personal experience about habits. He stated that it took a minimum of 21 days for old mental images to dissolve and new ones to become established. Psycho-Cybernetics, Maltz's book on behavior change, became a bestseller, and several self-help gurus drew inspiration from it. However, as his story spread, people began to shorten Maltz's quote to "It takes 21 days to form a new habit," even though he meant it as a minimum. This popular myth has no scientific basis. Just because it is repeated often enough in multiple venues does not make it true. Although the 21-day cycle is significant, Maltz's findings should not be taken as a fact, nor should they imply that it takes exactly 21 days to establish a new habit or break an old one. However, research suggests that this timeline is oversimplified. In a study by Lally et al. (2010)[1], published in the European Journal of Social Psychology, researchers found that the time required to form a habit can range from 18 to 254 days, with an average of around 66 days. The duration can vary based on factors such as the complexity of the habit, individual differences, and environmental influences.

Factors Influencing Habit Formation:

The Complexity of the Habit

The complexity of a habit can influence the time it takes to form a habit. Simple habits, such as drinking a glass of water each morning, may be established more quickly than complex habits involving multiple steps or requiring significant behavioral changes. One example of a complex habit is meal prepping. Meal prepping consists of planning and preparing multiple meals in advance, typically for several days or an entire week. This habit requires several steps, including meal planning, grocery shopping, ingredient preparation, cooking, portioning, and storing the meals. It also involves considering nutritional requirements, dietary preferences, and individual goals. Meal prepping can be time-consuming and may require organizational skills, cooking proficiency, and knowledge of food safety practices. Due to its multifaceted nature, meal prepping can take longer to establish as a habit than simpler habits, such as drinking a glass of water in the morning. However, once the habit is formed, it can provide numerous benefits, including saving time and money, promoting healthier eating habits, and reducing decision fatigue regarding meal choices.

Frequency and Consistency

Frequency and consistency play crucial roles in habit formation. The more frequently a behavior is performed, the more likely it becomes a habit. Consistency, on the other hand, refers to the regularity with which the behavior is performed over time. Daily repetition helps reinforce the habit cycle and strengthens the neural pathways associated with the behavior (Wood et al., 2019)[48]. By consistently repeating a behavior, individuals reinforce the neural pathways associated with that behavior, making it easier and more automatic over time.

Research has shown that higher frequency and consistent repetition of a behavior lead to more efficient habit formation. A study by Lally et al. (2010)[1] also revealed that missing a day or two of performing the behavior did not significantly impede habit formation. However, the consistent daily performance of the behavior was associated with faster habit development.

The relationship between frequency, consistency, and habit formation can be explained by the concept of *synaptic plasticity*. When a behavior is repeated, the synaptic connections between neurons involved in that behavior become stronger. This process, known as *long-term potentiation*, enhances the efficiency of neural communication and makes the behavior more automatic and ingrained.

Engaging in the desired behavior as frequently as possible and maintaining consistency over time is essential to maximize habit formation. Setting specific goals and creating a routine can help ensure regular engagement in the behavior. Additionally, strategies such as habit tracking, reminders, and accountability systems can aid in maintaining consistency.

Understanding the influence of frequency and consistency can guide individuals in effectively establishing new habits and promoting behavior change.

Environmental Factors

Our environment greatly influences habit formation. A supportive environment with cues and reminders can facilitate habit formation, while an environment filled with distractions or conflicting cues may hinder the process.

Environmental cues act as triggers for the habit loop and help establish the habit more effectively (Gardner, 2015)[49].

CHAPTER SUMMARY

Forming a habit is a gradual process that requires time, repetition, and consistency. While the idea of a 21-day rule is widespread, research suggests that habit formation can take much longer, with an average of around 66 days. The complexity of the habit, frequency, consistency of performance, and environmental factors all play a significant role in determining the timeline for habit formation. By understanding these factors, individuals can approach habit formation with realistic expectations and design strategies to cultivate new habits successfully.

Author's Note

Dear Readers,

Welcome to "*The Science of Habits - Why we do what we do and How to change it.*" This book is for those who have struggled with making lasting changes to their habits or are simply curious about the human brain and behavior.

Through this book, I aim to explore the science behind habits. Why do we develop habits in the first place? What role does our brain play in this process? Can we change our habits, and if so, how?

I have drawn from my personal experience as a physician health coach and have extensively researched the work of other experts in the field. The book is structured in a way that takes you from the fundamentals of habit formation to practical techniques that can help you change your behavior for the better.

While this book is aimed at a general audience, I have included scientific research studies to provide a grounded understanding of the concepts discussed. I hope you find the information presented in this book informative and actionable.

I am passionate about helping people make positive changes in their lives and believe that understanding the science of habits is crucial in this process. I would love to hear from you and your experiences with habit formation and change, and I wish you the best of luck in your journey towards shaping better habits.

Sincerely,

Adarsh Gupta

AdarshGupta.com

About Author

Adarsh Gupta, DO, is a physician, speaker, counselor, and consultant specializing in healthy habits coaching. Dr. Gupta has presented locally, regionally, nationally, and internationally on topics related to healthy lifestyle, weight management, metabolic disorders, and technology in medicine. He had authored numerous textbook chapters and journal articles. He is devoted to educating and motivating people to adopt and succeed in lifestyle modifications by promoting healthy eating habits and physical activity.

Resources

The Habit Cycle Worksheet.

The Habit Cycle Worksheet is a powerful tool designed to help individuals break bad habits and build new ones. It works by assisting individuals to create an alternate habit cycle, effectively replacing the old habit with a new one. This concept is explained in Chapter 5 while creating an alternate habit cycle for various bad habits.

This worksheet is structured so users can identify their current habit cycle and develop a suitable alternate one. It guides users in defining their goals and identifying triggers, cravings, actions, and rewards that help them build habits. Then, it allows them to develop an alternate habit cycle to build new healthy habits and reinforce those new habits until they become automatic.

This worksheet is an excellent tool for those who are committed to making lasting changes in their life and have struggled with breaking free from bad habits in the past.

You can download the Habit Cycle Worksheet free at https://adarshgupta.com/habitcycleworksheet/

References

1. Lally P, van Jaarsveld CHM, Potts HWW, Wardle J. How are habits formed: Modelling habit formation in the real world. *Eur J Soc Psychol*. 2010;40(6):998-1009. doi:10.1002/ejsp.674

2. Gardner B, Lally P, Wardle J. Making health habitual: the psychology of 'habit-formation' and general practice. *Br J Gen Pract*. 2012;62(605):664-666. doi:10.3399/bjgp12X659466

3. Wood W, Neal DT. A new look at habits and the habit-goal interface. *Psychol Rev*. 2007;114(4):843-863. doi:10.1037/0033-295X.114.4.843

4. Lepper MR, Greene D, Nisbett RE. Undermining children's intrinsic interest with extrinsic reward: A test of the "overjustification" hypothesis. *J Pers Soc Psychol*. 1973;28:129-137. doi:10.1037/h0035519

5. Vassiliadis P, Lete A, Duque J, Derosiere G. Reward timing matters in motor learning. *iScience*. 2022;25(5):104290. doi:10.1016/j.isci.2022.104290

6. Ersner-Hershfield H, Garton MT, Ballard K, Samanez-Larkin GR, Knutson B. Don't stop thinking about tomorrow: Individual differences in future self-continuity account for saving. *Judgm Decis Mak*. 2009;4(4):280-286.

7. Dickinson A, Balleine B. Motivational control of instrumental performance following a shift from thirst to hunger. *Q J Exp Psychol B*. 1990;42(4):413-431.

8. Aarts H, Verplanken B, van Knippenberg A. Habit and information use in travel mode choices. *Acta Psychol (Amst)*. 1997;96(1-2):1-14. doi:10.1016/S0001-6918(97)00008-5

9. Furr RM, Funder DC. A multimodal analysis of personal negativity. *J Pers Soc Psychol*. 1998;74(6):1580-1591. doi:10.1037/0022-3514.74.6.1580

10. Li MD, Burmeister M. New insights into the genetics of addiction. *Nat Rev Genet*. 2009;10(4):225-231. doi:10.1038/nrg2536

11. Graybiel AM, Rauch SL. Toward a Neurobiology of Obsessive-Compulsive Disorder. *Neuron*. 2000;28(2):343-347. doi:10.1016/S0896-6273(00)00113-6

12. Hölzel BK, Carmody J, Vangel M, et al. Mindfulness practice leads to increases in regional brain gray matter density. *Psychiatry Res*. 2011;191(1):36-43. doi:10.1016/j.pscychresns.2010.08.006

13. Sullivan EV, Pfefferbaum A. Neurocircuitry in alcoholism: a substrate of disruption and repair. *Psychopharmacology (Berl)*. 2005;180(4):583-594. doi:10.1007/s00213-005-2267-6

14. Yin HH, Knowlton BJ, Balleine BW. Lesions of dorsolateral striatum preserve outcome expectancy but disrupt habit formation in instrumental learning. *Eur J Neurosci*. 2004;19(1):181-189. doi:10.1111/j.1460-9568.2004.03095.x

15. Volkow ND, Wang GJ, Telang F, et al. Cocaine Cues and Dopamine in Dorsal Striatum: Mechanism of Craving in

Cocaine Addiction. *J Neurosci*. 2006;26(24):6583-6588. doi:10.1523/JNEUROSCI.1544-06.2006

16. Hyman SE, Malenka RC. Addiction and the brain: The neurobiology of compulsion and its persistence. *Nat Rev Neurosci*. 2001;2(10):695-703. doi:10.1038/35094560

17. Bierut LJ. Convergence of Genetic Findings for Nicotine Dependence and Smoking Related Diseases with Chromosome 15q24-25. *Trends Pharmacol Sci*. 2010;31(1):46-51. doi:10.1016/j.tips.2009.10.004

18. Huppertz C, Bartels M, van Beijsterveldt CEM, Boomsma DI, Hudziak JJ, de Geus EJC. The impact of shared environmental factors on exercise behavior from age 7 to 12. *Med Sci Sports Exerc*. 2012;44(10):2025-2032. doi:10.1249/MSS.0b013e31825d358e

19. Ryan RM, Deci EL. *Self-Determination Theory: Basic Psychological Needs in Motivation, Development, and Wellness*. Guilford Publications; 2018.

20. Ajzen I. The theory of planned behavior. *Organ Behav Hum Decis Process*. 1991;50(2):179-211. doi:10.1016/0749-5978(91)90020-T

21. Everitt BJ, Robbins TW. Neural systems of reinforcement for drug addiction: from actions to habits to compulsion. *Nat Neurosci*. 2005;8(11):1481-1489. doi:10.1038/nn1579

22. Bargh JA, Morsella E. The Unconscious Mind. *Perspect Psychol Sci*. 2008;3(1):73-79. doi:10.1111/j.1745-6916.2008.00064.x

23. Seger C, Spiering B. A Critical Review of Habit Learning and the Basal Ganglia. *Front Syst Neurosci*. 2011;5. Accessed April 27, 2023. https://www.frontiersin.org/articles/10.3389/fnsys.2011.00 066

24. Raichle ME, Snyder AZ. A default mode of brain function: A brief history of an evolving idea. *NeuroImage*. 2007;37(4):1083-1090. doi:10.1016/j.neuroimage.2007.02.041

25. Buckner RL, Carroll DC. Self-projection and the brain. *Trends Cogn Sci*. 2007;11(2):49-57. doi:10.1016/j.tics.2006.11.004

26. McLaughlin KA, Sheridan MA. Beyond Cumulative Risk: A Dimensional Approach to Childhood Adversity. *Curr Dir Psychol Sci*. 2016;25(4):239-245. doi:10.1177/0963721416655883

27. Tottenham N, Sheridan MA. A Review of Adversity, The Amygdala and the Hippocampus: A Consideration of Developmental Timing. *Front Hum Neurosci*. 2010;3:68. doi:10.3389/neuro.09.068.2009

28. Teicher MH, Samson JA. Childhood maltreatment and psychopathology: A case for ecophenotypic variants as clinically and neurobiologically distinct subtypes. *Am J Psychiatry*. 2013;170(10):1114-1133. doi:10.1176/appi.ajp.2013.12070957

29. Masten AS, Narayan AJ. Child development in the context of disaster, war, and terrorism: pathways of risk and resilience. *Annu Rev Psychol*. 2012;63:227-257. doi:10.1146/annurev-psych-120710-100356

30. Smith KS, Graybiel AM. Habit formation coincides with shifts in reinforcement representations in the sensorimotor striatum. *J Neurophysiol*. 2016;115(3):1487-1498. doi:10.1152/jn.00925.2015

31. Hofmann W, Luhmann M, Fisher RR, Vohs KD, Baumeister RF. Yes, but are they happy? Effects of trait self-control on affective well-being and life satisfaction. *J Pers*. 2014;82(4):265-277. doi:10.1111/jopy.12050

32. Salovey P, Mayer JD. Emotional intelligence. *Imagin Cogn Personal*. 1989;9:185-211. doi:10.2190/DUGG-P24E-52WK-6CDG

33. Tangney JP, Baumeister RF, Boone AL. High self-control predicts good adjustment, less pathology, better grades, and interpersonal success. *J Pers*. 2004;72(2):271-324. doi:10.1111/j.0022-3506.2004.00263.x

34. Astin JA, Shapiro SL, Eisenberg DM, Forys KL. Mind-body medicine: state of the science, implications for practice. *J Am Board Fam Pract*. 2003;16(2):131-147. doi:10.3122/jabfm.16.2.131

35. Lutz A, Slagter HA, Dunne JD, Davidson RJ. Attention regulation and monitoring in meditation. *Trends Cogn Sci*. 2008;12(4):163-169. doi:10.1016/j.tics.2008.01.005

36. Garland EL, Howard MO. Mindfulness-based treatment of addiction: current state of the field and envisioning the next wave of research. *Addict Sci Clin Pract*. 2018;13(1):14. doi:10.1186/s13722-018-0115-3

37. Kristeller JL, Wolever RQ. Mindfulness-based eating awareness training for treating binge eating disorder: the

conceptual foundation. *Eat Disord.* 2011;19(1):49-61. doi:10.1080/10640266.2011.533605

38. Bowen S, Witkiewitz K, Dillworth TM, et al. Mindfulness meditation and substance use in an incarcerated population. *Psychol Addict Behav J Soc Psychol Addict Behav.* 2006;20(3):343-347. doi:10.1037/0893-164X.20.3.343

39. Waveland Press - Behavior Modification in Applied Settings, Seventh Edition, by Alan E. Kazdin. Accessed April 28, 2023. https://www.waveland.com/browse.php?t=369

40. Gollwitzer PM, Sheeran P. Implementation intentions and goal achievement: A meta-analysis of effects and processes. In: *Advances in Experimental Social Psychology, Vol 38.* Advances in experimental social psychology. Elsevier Academic Press; 2006:69-119. doi:10.1016/S0065-2601(06)38002-1

41. Duckworth AL, Seligman MEP. Self-discipline outdoes IQ in predicting academic performance of adolescents. *Psychol Sci.* 2005;16:939-944. doi:10.1111/j.1467-9280.2005.01641.x

42. Xiang MQ, Liao JW, Huang JH, et al. Effect of a Combined Exercise and Dietary Intervention on Self-Control in Obese Adolescents. *Front Psychol.* 2019;10:1385. doi:10.3389/fpsyg.2019.01385

43. Baumeister RF, Gailliot M, DeWall CN, Oaten M. Self-regulation and personality: how interventions increase regulatory success, and how depletion moderates the effects of traits on behavior. *J Pers.* 2006;74(6):1773-1801. doi:10.1111/j.1467-6494.2006.00428.x

44. Wood JV, Perunovic WQE, Lee JW. Positive self-statements: power for some, peril for others. *Psychol Sci.* 2009;20(7):860-866. doi:10.1111/j.1467-9280.2009.02370.x

45. Falk EB, O'Donnell MB, Cascio CN, et al. Self-affirmation alters the brain's response to health messages and subsequent behavior change. *Proc Natl Acad Sci U S A.* 2015;112(7):1977-1982. doi:10.1073/pnas.1500247112

46. Hagger MS, Wood C, Stiff C, Chatzisarantis NLD. Ego depletion and the strength model of self-control: a meta-analysis. *Psychol Bull.* 2010;136(4):495-525. doi:10.1037/a0019486

47. Ghanizadeh A. Nail Biting; Etiology, Consequences and Management. *Iran J Med Sci.* 2011;36(2):73-79.

48. Wood W, Quinn JM, Kashy DA. Habits in everyday life: thought, emotion, and action. *J Pers Soc Psychol.* 2002;83(6):1281-1297.

49. Gardner B. A review and analysis of the use of "habit" in understanding, predicting, and influencing health-related behavior. *Health Psychol Rev.* 2015;9(3):277-295. doi:10.1080/17437199.2013.876238

Index